Misleading DNA Evidence

Misleading DNA Evidence: Reasons for Miscarriages of Justice

Peter Gill
Norwegian Institute of Public Health, Oslo,
University of Oslo, Norway

AMSTERDAM • BOSTON • HEIDELBERG • LONDON
NEW YORK • OXFORD • PARIS • SAN DIEGO
SAN FRANCISCO • SINGAPORE • SYDNEY • TOKYO
Academic Press is an imprint of Elsevier

ELSEVIER

Acquiring Editor: Elizabeth Brown
Editorial Project Manager: Joslyn Chaiprasert-Paguio
Project Manager: Mohana Natarajan

Academic Press is an imprint of Elsevier
32 Jamestown Road, London NW1 7BY, UK
The Boulevard, Langford Lane, Kidlington, Oxford, OX5 1GB, UK
Radarweg 29, PO Box 211, 1000 AE Amsterdam, The Netherlands
225 Wyman Street, Waltham, MA 02451, USA
525 B Street, Suite 1900, San Diego, CA 92101-4495, USA

British Library Cataloguing in Publication Data
A catalogue record for this book is available from the British Library

Library of Congress Cataloging-in-Publication Data
A catalog record for this book is available from the Library of Congress

ISBN: 978-0-12-417214-2

For information on all Academic Press publications
visit our website at store.elsevier.com

Working together
to grow libraries in
developing countries

www.elsevier.com • www.bookaid.org

DEDICATION

This book is for my wife Christine. With tolerance and patience, she has supported and encouraged me for many years.

ACKNOWLEDGMENTS

I am grateful to all of my colleagues for their help and support during this project, in particular, Hinda Haned, Thore Egeland, Oyvind Bleka and Jonathan Whitaker have all provided me with valuable advice and comments.

The preparation of this book has received funding from the European Union seventh Framework Programme (FP7/2007-2013) under grant agreement no. 285487 (EUROFORGEN-NoE) and it contributes towards the deliverable: "A protocol to describe best practice at the crime-scene".

My career began 32 years ago at the Home Office Central Research Establishment (Aldermaston, UK) in 1982; I stayed with the Forensic Science Service until 2008. I became Professor of Forensic Genetics at the University of Oslo, Norway and in 2011 accepted a concurrent position at the Norwegian Institute of Public Health. I have published more than 180 peer-reviewed papers and these have been cited by other authors of scientific papers more than 12,800 times (lifetime h-index = 63). I am chair of the DNA commission of the International Society of Forensic Genetics (ISFG); co-chair of the "Analysis, Methods and Interpretation" subgroup of the European Network of Forensic Science Institutes (ENFSI) DNA working group; and a member of the Euroforgen network of excellence, which is funded by the European Union. I was awarded ISFG Scientific Prize in 2013.

While at the Forensic Science Service, in 1985 I developed the DNA extraction methods for forensic samples and used the results to publish the first demonstration of forensic DNA profiling with Alec Jeffreys. In the 1990s, I led the team that developed the modern genotyping methods of short tandem repeat (multiplexed) STR analysis. The methods were subsequently introduced worldwide and were used to create the world's first national DNA database in the United Kingdom, along with interpretation and search protocols. In 1993, I was formally approached by the Russian Federation to lead a joint project to analyze the putative remains of the last Tsar of Russia—the first historical mystery to be solved by DNA analysis. Although the results were considered controversial at the time, in the following decades, subsequent analysis by others verified the original conclusions. The claim of Anna Anderson to be the duchess Anastasia was also investigated by DNA analysis and shown to be false. In the year 2000, I led the team that developed a new ultrasensitive method of DNA typing—called low copy number—also considered to be controversial at the time. An interpretation framework was concurrently developed, and once again the methods have since been adopted worldwide. Since then, I have specialized in developing statistical methods to interpret complex DNA profiles and have supported open-source initiatives. I have given evidence in several high-profile trials and courts of appeal, both in the United States (Frye hearing in New York) and in the United Kingdom, including the Omagh bombing trial, where the judge summarized: "In my view it was extremely fortunate that the prosecution decided late in the day to call Dr Gill as his evidence greatly helped to inform and bring some objectivity to the debate." The motivation for this book arose from a meeting in Rome that was organized by Vince Pascali in 2012, entitled: "The hidden side of DNA profiles." I have carried out a deep analysis of a number of poorly reported cases, which are described in the book. Bearing in mind that this represents a tiny snapshot of current practice, there is little doubt in my mind that misinterpretation of DNA profiling evidence may cause miscarriages of justice. My purpose is to provide some clarity—in particular to urge scientists, lawyers, judges, and their policy makers to engage in debate and to examine their existing practices.

FOREWORD

Forensic DNA testing, which is arguably the most significant advance in forensic science in the twentieth century, began with a publication in the prestigious journal *Nature* in December 1985. While we appropriately honor Professor Alec Jeffreys as the father of forensic DNA analysis, Dr. Peter Gill, the first author of this initial paper, has been a thought leader in many areas of forensic DNA methods and interpretation over the past several decades.

In my opinion, over the past three decades *no one has done more* to advance forensic DNA analysis and interpretation than Peter Gill. He has been part of every major development in the field. A few of the articles that come to mind include the early exploration of short tandem repeats in 1993 (published in *PCR Methods & Applications*), use of DNA to solve the Romanov historical mystery in 1994 (published in *Nature Genetics*), the establishment of the first national DNA database in 1995 (based on concepts originally published in 1990 in *Electrophoresis*), the introduction of mixture interpretation techniques in 1998 and low-copy number procedures in 2000 (published in *Forensic Science International*), recognition of the potential impact of DNA contamination in 2004 (published in the *Journal of Forensic Science*), simulation of the DNA testing process in order to understand it better in 2005 (published in *Nucleic Acids Research*), and development of recommendations on probabilistic genotyping methods in 2012 (published in *Forensic Science International: Genetics*). His work has longevity as well as a breadth and depth unequaled in the field. He has had and continues to have real impact with his visionary work.

This book furthers the reach and impact of Dr. Gill, who is now a professor of forensic genetics at the University of Oslo in Norway. *Misleading DNA Evidence* contains five primary sections: (1) a definition of "trace DNA," (2) a review of some causes of miscarriages of justice when there is an oversimplification of evidence interpretation, (3) a framework to guide trace DNA evidence interpretation with 13 recommendations, (4) a discussion of uses and abuses of DNA databases, and (5) an interesting review and discussion of the case investigating the death of Meredith Kercher where Amanda Knox and others were accused and convicted by an Italian court.

Misleading DNA Evidence should be required reading for all forensic DNA analysts so that they can better appreciate the limitations of the powerful technique that they wield with DNA testing results that have become increasingly more sensitive in recent years. Police investigators and members of the legal community who rely on DNA evidence to make decisions should also read this book as it provides an important word of caution on the challenges surrounding DNA interpretation as detection methods have become more sensitive. The text reminds us that just because a DNA profile can now be obtained from a few cells does not mean that the source of the profile is relevant to the crime event being investigated. Transfer, persistence, and mixtures are all possible and can confound interpretation of the results obtained. Likewise, readers are reminded that the absence of evidence is not the evidence of absence and so *not* obtaining a DNA profile does not mean that a potential suspect is not associated with the crime under investigation and therefore may not be truly innocent.

Professor Gill notes the true challenge he is trying to address near the beginning of his book: "to refrain from overstepping boundaries of knowledge—[in other words] to imply that the evidence has more meaning than it really does—this is how miscarriages of justice occur." These miscarriages of justice can occur due to what he describes as "the compounded error effect" from "the association fallacy," "the hidden perpetrator effect," "the naïve investigator effect," and the "swamping effect."

In my interactions with Peter over the years, I have found him to be a forward thinker and an excellent scientist. This book serves as a reminder and demonstration of Peter Gill's work ethic, his scientific integrity, and the positive impact he has had over the years on the field of forensic DNA typing. Hopefully, the message of his book will be understood and potential miscarriages of justice avoided as these principles are applied to strengthen the field of forensic science.

John M. Butler, Ph.D.
NIST Fellow & Special Assistant to the
Director for Forensic Science
National Institute of Standards and Technology
Gaithersburg, Maryland, USA

It is nearly 30 years since the first demonstration of DNA profiling in forensic science. Since then, the technique has evolved remarkably. In the early days, only large "visible" crime stains (e.g., blood, semen) were analyzed. This was imposed by the relatively poor sensitivity relative to today's standards. There is an inherent advantage to the interpretation of macro-DNA samples, in that it is much easier to deduce the relevance of a supposed crime stain to the crime event itself. From the perspective of a court, the fact that a DNA profile may match a defendant is of secondary interest to the questions: "how" and "when" did the DNA transfer take place? For a defendant to be found guilty, a court must be convinced that the DNA profile is associated with the crime event itself. The forensic scientist attempts to apply "deductive logic" in order to *associate* the DNA profile with some other aspect of the case—it is not the "fact" of a matching DNA profile that is of primary interest, rather it is the "context" or the "relevance" of the DNA profile to the crime event itself. To make deductive inferences, a chain of associations is implied. For example, the DNA profile may be found along with a positive test for blood. The scientist may deduce that the origin of the DNA is from blood—an association is made. The confirmation of a body fluid "source" is often sufficient to imply an "activity"—if blood is present, then the prosecution may imply that the defendant or victim bled at the crime scene; alternatively, the confirmation of semen may imply sexual assault. Once these associations have been accepted, the court's task to decide the ultimate issue of guilt/innocence is a short step to take.

Associations are necessary for any deductions to be made. In recent years, the sensitivity of DNA profiling has steadily increased, so that now the analysis of just a "handful" of cells is not only possible, but also routine in most forensic laboratories. This has been made possible by the introduction of new multiplexes by manufacturers (these are biochemical systems used to detect DNA profiles), along with new highly sensitive detection platforms.

However, as the sensitivity of DNA profiling technology increases, there is a parallel increase in the uncertainty of associations. This is because DNA is everywhere in the environment. It can be transferred passively, e.g., by touching a surface, or by secondary transfer, mediated by a person other than the defendant. DNA will persist indefinitely in a dry environment, hence there is no implicit information attached to the DNA profile that gives a clue to the "how" and "when" transfer occurred.

To avoid false associations leading to false deductive logic, it is necessary for scientists to actively consider all possible methods of transfer: before the crime event—innocent transfer or background contamination; after the crime event—investigator mediated contamination. The identification of a DNA profile and body fluid are two separate tests. The association of the body fluid *with* the DNA profile is not implicit. The strength of the evidence expressed as the chance of a random man match or a likelihood ratio cannot be simply transposed to express an equivalent strength of evidence under the assumption that the DNA profile originated from a given body fluid; the uncertainty reduces the strength of the evidence, but this is not always taken into consideration when expert evidence is provided. The uncertainties increase as we consider the "activity" that produced the DNA transfer—as before, the DNA statistic cannot be transposed.

The book is structured into a number of chapters:

The first chapter discusses a definition of "trace-DNA" and proceeds to explain the main types of contamination and its impact. There follows a description of causes of miscarriages of justice: the association fallacy; the hidden perpetrator effect; the compounded error effect; cognitive biases—especially confirmation bias. The role of the forensic scientist is clarified within the context of a "statement of limitations" intended to anchor the evidence at a level that can be supported in a strict scientific sense, so that speculative "expert-opinion" is avoided.

The second chapter investigates the causes of miscarriages of justice by reference to several verified and unverified examples, showing how mistakes occur at every level of the criminal justice system: the investigator; the scientist; lawyers; the judge; the jury are all susceptible to an over-simplistic interpretation of evidence that is primarily driven by a family of cognitive errors.

In the third chapter, a detailed framework is provided to interpret "trace-DNA" evidence. Recovery of DNA from underneath fingernails is used as an example since there has been much research into the investigation of transfer and persistence of DNA in this type of evidence. The exemplar framework can be expanded to other evidence types.

There has been much debate on the use of national DNA databases in crime investigation, but the "debate" was never properly resolved. In the fourth chapter, it is shown that databases can be misused or misunderstood to provide an impression that the DNA evidence is highly probative in a given case. However, when the other non-DNA evidence is neutral, or exculpatory, it is demonstrated that the DNA evidence can be overweighted in relation to the non-DNA evidence. This is because the former is expressed numerically (e.g., one in one billion), whereas the non-DNA evidence is expressed verbally, without statistics. I call this the "swamping effect". There are numbers of proposals put forward to redress the balance.

The final chapter brings together the various strands—using the case of "Death of Meredith Kercher" to illustrate the various principles and cognitive biases explained in previous chapters. A list of recommendations is provided.

Books are often static entities, but I would like this to be a vehicle to facilitate discussion between all of the participants of the criminal justice system and their policy makers. It has been prepared as a contribution to a deliverable towards: "A protocol that describes best practice at crime scene", under the auspices of the EU-funded, Euroforgen-Network of Excellence, http://www.euroforgen.eu/. The European Network of Forensic Institutes (ENFSI) is concurrently running a project entitled "The development and implementation of an ENFSI standard for reporting evaluative forensic evidence", http://www.enfsi.eu/projects/monopoly-programmes-mp/mp2010. The ideas also contribute to this programme. They were recently discussed at an ENFSI meeting in Tbilisi, Georgia. I am very pleased that a general consensus is already emerging within the scientific community. I am sure that I will need to expand, modify, update, and consolidate some of my ideas. I welcome comments to peterd.gill@gmail.com and I will post updates on my Web site, https://sites.google.com/site/peterdgill/.

CONTENTS

CHAPTER 1

Definitions: Contamination and Interpretation

1.1 HISTORICAL

The original DNA profiling technique developed in 1985 had relatively low sensitivity. It was limited to the analysis of large *visible* crime stains that were at least 1 cm in diameter. Improvements facilitated by the widespread adoption of the polymerase chain reaction (PCR) method gradually increased the sensitivity to the point that only a few cells were required in an assay (Gill et al., 2000). At first this development was regarded as controversial, but now, the analysis of "trace-DNA"[1] has become routine. This book is about the interpretation of DNA profiles derived from "trace-DNA" evidence.

1.2 DEFINITION OF "TRACE-DNA"

The term "trace-DNA" was used in a recent review by van Oorschot et al. (2010):

> Trace-DNA samples may be defined as any sample which falls below recommended thresholds at any stage of the analysis.

I have modified this definition simply because this type of analysis is now universal. It has been motivated by the introduction of new biochemistry and

---

[1] Encompasses "low-level" DNA, "low-template," or low-copy-number DNA.

instrumentation over recent years. Manufacturers compete with each other to develop the most sensitive methods and forensic scientists readily adopt the new systems, along with protocols that now standardize tests.

Therefore, I have altered Oorschots definition of "trace-DNA" to take account of this change in practice. The key to the definition is whether a DNA profile is meaningful within the context of the "Locard's exchange principle": "every contact leaves a trace" and its implied extension to: "every perpetrator leaves a trace."

Accordingly, I have redefined as follows:

Trace-DNA is defined as any sample where there is uncertainty that it may be associated with the crime event itself—so that it is possible that the transfer may have occurred before *the crime event (innocent transfer) or* after *the crime event (investigator mediated).*

The definition is deliberately vague: it hinges upon an assessment of the *relevance* of a "trace-DNA" profile to the crime event which is considered in the context of a "statement of limitations" originally published in 2001 and reproduced below.

1.2.1 "Trace-DNA" Evidence: Statement of Limitations (Gill, 2001)

This is the "starting" position:

1. Although a DNA profile has been obtained, it is possible neither to identify the type of cells from which the DNA originated, nor to state *when* the cells were deposited.
2. It is not possible to make any conclusion about *transfer and persistence* of DNA in this case. It is not possible to estimate when the suspect last wore the [watch],[2] if it is his DNA.
3. Because the DNA test is very sensitive, it is not unexpected to find mixtures. If the potential origins of DNA profiles cannot be identified, it does not necessarily follow that they are relevant to this case, since transfer of cells can occur as a result of casual contact.

The definition of "trace-DNA" will encompass a large proportion of crime samples that are currently processed within DNA laboratories. It will include

---

[2]This statement was originally used in relation to DNA evidence found on a watch found at a crime scene.

all low-level DNA profiles, for which there is no concurrent body fluid that has been identified with certainty (Section 1.5).

1.2.2 Assessment of "Trace-DNA" Evidence in the Context of the Case: "The List of Possibilities"

With some cases (examples described later in the book) it will not be possible for a scientist to go beyond the "statement of limitations." The prosecution will nevertheless "push" the scientist to associate the "trace-DNA" evidence with the crime event "activity"; the challenge is to refrain from overstepping boundaries of knowledge—i.e., to imply that the evidence has more meaning than it really does—this is how miscarriages of justice occur.

The second step is to explain *all* of the different possibilities describing *how* a "trace-DNA" may be transferred, without expressing any preference. The list should be fully inclusive—just because the scientist believes that a particular mode of transfer is remote, it is not a reason to omit it from the list of possibilities:

1. The "trace-DNA" profile was transferred during the crime event itself.
2. The "trace-DNA" profile was part of the background contamination of the crime scene (innocent transfer).
3. The "trace-DNA" profile was a *post* crime scene contamination event (investigator-mediated contamination).

The list can be subdivided or expanded further to take account of the specific case circumstances. The next question evaluates whether the various possibilities can be ranked in order of "likelihood." This is the most difficult part of the exercise and much caution is required to take the interpretation toward an opinion on the "activity" that led to the transfer of the "trace-DNA" profile. Whether this is possible is very case specific, but provided that there are sufficient experimental data that are relevant, underpinned by peer-reviewed literature, and provided that there is a good understanding about the background and investigator-mediated contamination, then it may be possible to provide some further meaning to the "trace-DNA" evidence.

Chapter 3 provides a detailed exemplar framework to assess "trace-DNA" evidence from underneath fingernails. This is probably the best-researched evidence type; probabilistic assessments can be made to describe the likelihood of a transfer event via each of the possibilities. The research to date shows the inherent unpredictability of DNA transfer at the crime scene that is influenced by numerous variables which are difficult to evaluate and to quantify.

Sometimes forensic scientists may try to find meaning in the absence of a DNA profile, to prove a negative: e.g., "Mr X was not in the room because I could not find his DNA." This is a specious argument. Absence of evidence is not evidence of absence.

1.3 A DISCUSSION ON CONTAMINATION

DNA is everywhere in the environment. A DNA profile cannot be interpreted under the strict confines of "Locard's exchange principle" as there are several alternative transfer methods other than direct "contact." DNA can be transferred from one place to another—either by other people or in aerosol suspension, as house dust, composed of dead-skin-cells, for example, first demonstrated by Toothman et al. (2008) who concluded:

> even though anti-contamination measures may be in place at a crime scene and in the laboratory, trace DNA derived from dust in the vicinity of other evidence is capable of producing signals higher than background noise in STR analyses.

1.3.1 Mechanisms of DNA Transfer

There are three different mechanisms whereby DNA may be transferred between surfaces, people, or objects. These methods are exhaustive (i.e., I can't think of another method), but they are not mutually exclusive—more than one mechanism may occur either simultaneously or at different times.

1. *Direct transfer*: Directly touching a surface object or person. No intermediary is involved.
2. *Aerosol transfer*: Transfer to a person, surface, or object is achieved without an intermediary. Examples are exhaling or speaking where saliva spray is transferred from a person to a surface, object or another person. Another example is skin cells which are continually shed into the environment. An intermediary is not involved with this method of transfer.
3. *Indirect transfer (or secondary transfer)*: Where a DNA profile initially deposited either by direct means or by aerosol is transferred via an intermediary who touches the DNA profile and transfers "sticky-DNA" to another surface, object, or person. The definition includes transfer between two objects that physically touch each other. Multiple transfer events, where a DNA profile may be transferred by indirect method more than once may occur. An intermediary is always involved with indirect transfer.

1.3.2 Relevance of DNA Transfer at the Crime Scene

It is usually necessary to interpret the *relevance* of the DNA profiles recovered from the crime scene in relation to the crime event itself. Here, DNA transfer is described as either *active* (relevant) or *passive* (not relevant):

1.3.2.1 Active Transfer

Active transfer is associated with direct transfer of DNA during the crime event itself—e.g., by sexual assault and transfer of sperm to the victim; a victim scratches an assailant and a DNA profile is transferred underneath fingernails (Chapter 3).

1.3.2.2 Passive Transfer

1. Passive transfer results in the "background" distribution of DNA profiles that pre-exists the crime scene. The population of DNA profiles is derived by any of the following mechanisms which are described above:
   - Direct transfer
   - Aerosol transfer
   - Indirect transfer
2. Once the crime scene is established, the investigator may inadvertently act as a vector to passively transfer DNA within the immediate environment (Section 1.3.7)
3. These risks extend to collection of items, their packaging, examination in the laboratory, storage, re-examination where indirect passive transfer may act to redistribute DNA profiles within and between items of evidence (Section 1.3.3).

1.3.2.3 Summary of DNA Transfer Methods

In summary, there are six exhaustive methods or "states" to describe DNA transfer, as listed below:

1. *Active, direct*: Describes relevant transfer from the perpetrator at the time of the crime event.
2. *Active, indirect*: This "state" is probably not significant since it describes relevant secondary transfer at the time of the crime event.
3. *Active, aerosol*: For example, transfer from perpetrator via saliva spray from exhaling, shouting.
4. *Passive, direct*: Innocent touching, not associated with the crime event.
5. *Passive, indirect*: Innocent secondary transfer.
6. *Passive aerosol*: Innocent transfer via speaking, exhaling, skin cells.

For any recovered "trace-DNA" profile, the actual method will not be known with certainty.

1.3.3 Aerosol Transfer at the Crime Scene and Between Packaged Items

- Where airborne-DNA is transferred to a surface. It has been demonstrated that speaking or coughing will result in transfer of DNA up to 180 cm distance from the contributor (Finnebraaten et al., 2008; Port et al., 2006; Rutty et al., 2003). It has been previously proposed that airborne passive transfer is responsible for contamination of plasticware (supposedly DNA free) (Gill et al., 2010), either in the laboratory itself or at manufacturing source. DNA can be recovered from "house-dust," hence it would be expected to be in suspension in the air. However, from the limited amount of work that has been carried out (Vandewoestyne et al., 2011; Witt et al., 2009), this does not appear to be a major mechanism of cross-contamination.
- Aerosol transfer has been convincingly demonstrated to occur between case items that are loosely packed together, e.g., heavily contaminated blood on clothing will transfer to other objects that may be packed separately (Goray et al., 2012a). Classified as "passive transfer" as it is not physically mediated by an individual. Visible encrusted body fluid stains readily produce aerosol flakes upon disturbance and this is particularly "dangerous" within the confines of loosely packaged material. This phenomenon will be particularly relevant to "cold" cases; these are unsolved crimes, where the items were collected, stored, and examined under conditions that did not anticipate highly sensitive DNA profiling methods. As technology progresses, these cases are sometimes reanalyzed in an attempt to discover perpetrators. Each time the case is re-examined, the risks are increased because of the added disturbances. If items from a known suspect have been kept together with questioned items from a case, then it is to be expected that cross-contamination will occur between them. The "statement of limitations" (Section 1.2.1) will apply to all such cases; the possibility of cross-contamination would rank highly (see Section 2.3.3).

1.3.4 Indirect (Secondary Transfer) at the Crime Scene

There are excellent experimental designs to illustrate the risks of secondary transfer described by a series of papers by Goray et al. (2010a,b, 2012b). These articles also serve as reviews of the literature, not reproduced here. These papers show that secondary transfer is dependent upon the type of surface (porous or smooth), and also whether the samples are wet vs. dry. It was shown that porous/dry samples were less likely to transfer DNA than smooth/wet samples. Friction between two surfaces aided secondary transfer.Skin cell transfer is of particular interest, since this is the cell type that is most likely to be inadvertently transferred at crime scenes. Goray et al. (2010a) showed that just 2 ng of skin cell DNA were required to transfer 1 ng to be retrieved from another surface. A review of the literature showed that a handprint deposited between 0 and 385 ng of DNA—i.e., there was usually more than enough to be realistically implicated in the possibility of secondary transfer. In addition, it was shown that latex gloves worn by investigators at crime scenes are "high risk" in this respect (Poy and van Oorschot, 2006; Szkuta et al., 2013) (Section 5.13.3). It is important to note that the published literature has focussed on retrieval of DNA profiles of 1 ng or more, which is reflective of "traditional" DNA profiling methods. However, the examples that are examined in this book include the retrieval of much lower amounts of DNA—these are typically low-level, partial DNA profiles that are routinely reported using enhanced PCR amplification cycles, or the new, more sensitive multiplexes and platforms that are currently utilized.

Since the new methodologies are in the region 20 times more sensitive than those previously considered, there is an urgent need to carry out new research, following the experimental design of Goray et al., in order to properly quantify the risks of the new technologies that have already been implemented—Ballantyne et al. (2013) reported greatly increased detection of background contamination on surfaces and equipment associated with laboratory analysis. Profiles that are demonstrably low-level, partial, and in admixture with other contributors should always be considered as potential background contamination.

1.3.5 The "Natural Environment" of the Crime Scene

The "natural environment" of the "crime scene" is defined by background DNA distribution that existed *before* the crime event. After the crime event, a crime scene is established. The purpose of the investigation is to determine the differences between the DNA distributions of the "natural environment" from the new distributions imposed by the crime event itself. Apart from the complications arising from the "background contamination," investigators may themselves contaminate the crime scene—this is called "investigator-mediated contamination." The transfer mechanisms were described in Section 1.3.1.

Background contamination is unavoidable and must always be taken into consideration when a crime scene is investigated.[3]

Investigator-mediated contamination is theoretically avoidable, but in practice it will be difficult to preclude the possibility. The two main types of contamination are summarized below.

1.3.6 Background Contamination

People who inhabit premises, along with their visitors, will shed their DNA so that it will be all pervasive in the environment. It will be present on surfaces as "sticky-DNA" and in aerosol as skin cells which form a component of "house dust" or saliva spray generated by exhaling or speaking.[4] It can be propagated either by passive or active transfer as outlined above. Background contaminating DNA remains intact for months, if not years after deposition, provided that the environment is dry and undisturbed (Raymond et al., 2009).

1.3.7 Investigator-Mediated Contamination

This kind of contamination is outside the "natural environment" of the case. It is mediated by investigators who unwittingly contaminate the crime scene with their own DNA—this is usually detected if investigator DNA databases are kept. However, the second form of investigator-mediated contamination is more serious—disposable paper suits and gloves intended to prevent DNA transfer from the wearer may inadvertently transfer "sticky-DNA" from one part of the crime scene to another (e.g., by not changing gloves in between examination of items). Once items are packaged and transported for analysis, e.g., a knife or some clothing, "aerosol DNA" can redistribute itself both within and between poorly packaged evidential items (Goray et al., 2012a). Laboratory contamination includes contamination of plasticware and reagents, either at the manufacturing source or within the laboratory itself (Gill et al., 2010; Tamariz et al., 2006).

1.3.8 A Theoretical Example to Illustrate the Various Transfer Mechanisms

Routes of contamination relative to a time line are illustrated in Figure 1.1. At a premises, several people cohabit a house. They and their visitors shed DNA by passive transfer. Three profiles are deposited by individuals

---

[3]Currently, there is insufficient research and guidance to recommend exactly how this should be done, but I envisage a system of random sampling by transects taken from the vicinity of the crime scene.
[4]This is why investigators wear face masks.

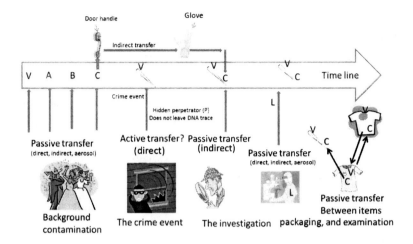

Figure 1.1 Routes of contamination relative to a time line. See text for explanation.

V, A, B, respectively. Individual C is an irregular visitor to the house. He has deposited his DNA on a door handle of V's bedroom. While A, B, C were all absent from the house, there is a break-in entry. The victim (V) is clubbed to death in her bedroom with a baseball bat that belongs to her and is verified to be the murder weapon. As the victim fell face down onto the floor, she bled profusely from her nose, staining her T-shirt. A crime scene is established. Before the DNA evidence is evaluated, C is a suspect since A and B both testify that V and C had a heated argument the previous day at the flat—this is not disputed. C says he has never seen or touched the baseball bat. As there is no visible body fluid, all of the evidence recovered is "trace-DNA." A DNA profile matches V. This is explained either as passive transfer before the crime event, or active transfer during the crime event and a DNA profile matching C is found on the handle. Unknown to everyone, the scientific investigator failed to change latex gloves after entering the room—he touched the door handle to open the door and then touched the murder weapon. Passive transfer (contamination) was responsible for the only visible profile from C. The "hidden perpetrator effect" (Section 1.5.2) has occurred—where the profile from the perpetrator is absent.[5] Suspect C visited the premises the night before the murder. Since he denies touching the baseball bat, the discovery of his DNA profile on the handle immediately implicates him in the crime. When apprehended by

---

[5]Note: there is no guarantee that the perpetrator will deposit DNA at the crime scene; or if he does a mixed profile may be present—if the latter occurs it is possible the perpetrator is classified as "unknown" if absent from the national DNA database, leaving C as the only "known" profile—also see the naïve investigator effect (Section 4.8.1).

police he was wearing recently laundered clothing which was taken away for forensic examination. The victim's T-shirt is also taken to the same laboratory. The items are packaged separately, but stored together in a large paper bag.

The encrusted blood stains of victim's T-shirt have an opportunity to passively transfer "trace-DNA" profiles between poorly packaged items and during the examination itself. Consequently, "trace-DNA" passively transferred from V may be discovered on C's clean T-shirt, implicating him further in the crime if misinterpreted as active transfer.

Compare the scenario outlined above with the "death of Meredith Kercher" example: Chapter 5.

1.3.9 Confirmation Bias

Confirmation bias begins with the scientist/investigator "searching for evidence" to discover a perpetrator of some offence. "Locard's exchange principle": "every contact leaves a trace" drives the "expectation" that the discovery of a DNA profile must be significant in relation to crime. This gives the investigator an illusion of objectivity where none may exist. If a DNA profile is discovered and a match with a man is obtained, he becomes a suspect, and then the machinery of justice places him center stage. The interpretation of the evidence is anchored on the suspect. The DNA profile may match the suspect—but how confident can we be that the DNA profile that has been recovered is *relevant* to the crime event itself? What is the probability that the transfer method was "active direct" (Section 1.3.2.3)?

Confirmation Bias

Confirmation bias is a well-characterized phenomenon: the tendency to search for or interpret information in a way that confirms one's preconceptions. In addition, individuals may discredit information that does not support their views (http://en.wikipedia.org/wiki/Cognitive_bias#cite_note-26).

1.3.10 Conclusion

Laboratories take extra precautions to prevent cross-transfer *within* the laboratory environment.[6] The same processes must occur unrestricted within

---

[6]By wearing protective clothing; filtering air into the laboratory; by frequent decontamination of surfaces and equipment.

the crime scene environment. The crime scene DNA distribution can only be ascertained after the crime event itself. The interpretation of the totality of the evidence may be compromised by a failure to understand the DNA distribution that existed before the crime event, i.e., the distribution of DNA observed at the crime scene is a combination of pre-existing background profiles along with crime-event-specific profiles (that may or may not present).

1.4 WHY DO MISCARRIAGES OF JUSTICE OCCUR?

The process of interpretation is not limited to the presentation of a simple statistic to the court. The forensic scientist is often requested to provide some additional meaning—e.g., how or when was the DNA transferred? The extent to which this evaluation occurs varies according to the jurisdiction, but taking the UK as an example, it is commonplace to assign a strength of evidence that is not restricted to the simple fact of the DNA profile.

1.4.1 Courts Sometimes Confuse "Expert Opinion" to Be the Equivalent of "Scientific Evidence"

Courts may be unable to tell the difference between "expert opinion" and "scientific evidence." The scientific method was developed more than 300 years ago and is largely attributed to Sir Isaac Newton (Section 4.31). However, it is clear that some forensic evidence provided to courts is better described as "speculation" rather than science. To proceed to a "scientific evaluation" of the speculative "belief," experimentation is always required in order to prove or disprove a hypothesis. A scientifically valid "expert opinion" must be based upon experimental design and preferably underpinned by peer-review. If peer review does not exist,[7] then a body of data that *can be* independently peer reviewed might suffice instead. There are many examples in the following chapters where the scientific method is not followed, yet courts continually fail to recognize the significance; the default position seems to follow that provided the person is recognized as an expert,[8] then everything he/she states must be "scientific evidence." However, as explained above, this premise is incorrect.

Even where experimentation exists, forensic scientists have to relate the results to a given case. Given that case circumstances are often highly

---

[7]There may be argument that the work is not published as it is not sufficiently interesting to a journal.
[8]The definition of an "expert" in the UK is very loose since there is no formal requirement to be qualified in the area in which he/she gives evidence.

specific it may not be possible to generalize experiments that have been carried out using different sets of conditions. In practice, generalizations are difficult, unless they relate to a particular type of evidence. One of the better researched areas is "DNA under fingernails," where a body of data can be used to make inferences about transfer and persistence of DNA profiles (Chapter 3).

To summarize: "expert-opinion" and "scientific evidence" are not the same. Scientific evidence requires experimentation to test a hypothesis. If this is missing, then the "evidence" is speculation. For a scientist, in the absence of relevant experimental output, the default position is always provided by the "statement of limitations" (Section 1.2.1).

1.5 SOME FALLACIES AND ERRORS OF THINKING

To infer when or how evidence was deposited is reliant upon additional information. Consider a case of rape—the association of sperm cells with the DNA profile of the suspect is necessary to prove rape occurred. If the DNA came from skin cells, there is no proof of the alleged activity. The DNA profile by itself provides no additional clues of its specific cellular origin. The question remains about the confidence with which an association of a DNA profile with sperm cells is valid, compared to a proposal that the DNA originated from an alternative source such as skin cells?

Second, the impact of background contaminating DNA to confuse the evidential significance is a major consideration. Background DNA is all pervasive in the environment (Toothman et al., 2008)—the lower the amount of starting template, the higher the probability that a contamination event will be unknowingly detected.[9] In addition, the forensic scientist deals primarily with body fluids that are often difficult to identify, especially if they too are low level. Interpretation is complicated if there are mixtures of body fluids or other sources. Tests are presumptive and not definitive.

There are common causes to miscarriages of justice. The following summarizes the principle reasons, that are expanded in subsequent sections of the book.

---

[9] It is important to recognize that this has nothing to do with low template definitions based on arbitrary limits of DNA quantity.

1.5.1 The Association Fallacy

The Association Fallacy

The strength of the evidence of the DNA profile may be wrongly transposed to include a defined body fluid such as blood or semen in the calculation. The "association fallacy" is introduced to describe the "automatic" and absolute assumption that a DNA profile has come from a body fluid on the strength of presumptive or RNA tests, verified by "expert opinion." However, the observation of a body fluid and the detection of a DNA profile are two separate tests. It cannot be implied with certainty that the body fluid and the DNA have the same source. The fallacy also describes wrongful association of the presence of a body fluid, such as sperm with an activity (sexual assault in this example).

With the error of the "association fallacy" it is assumed that there is a *dependency* between two observations or events. The opposite version is the assumption of *independence* which is also an error that can lead to miscarriages of justice—the classic example identified in the Sally Clark case (Hill, 2004) was the wrongful assumption that two natural cot-deaths from the same mother were independent events and the combined probability was vanishingly small. A conviction of infanticide resulted since the defence alternative was described as remote. However the reverse is true, a single cot-death makes a second event more likely—the two events are not independent of each other—the conviction was eventually overturned. The message is clear—neither dependence nor independence should be assumed unless there is experimental evidence in support. Expert opinion has to be distanced from personal "beliefs" or "leaps of faith" in order to be objective.

The prevalence of contamination can greatly affect interpretation of evidence. However, not all contamination events result in error. Often, a contaminant is a minor component of a mixture and provided the true donor is present as a contributor (although we can't tell if this is true just by observing a DNA profile), then it does not adversely affect the interpretation.

1.5.2 The Hidden Perpetrator Effect

The most dangerous aspect of contamination occurs when insufficient DNA is recovered from an actual perpetrator. Now consider the contaminant to be the only visible profile. Using an example of sexual assault, there is an "expectation" driven by "confirmation bias" that the DNA has come from the culprit. If the database trawl identifies an individual, he now becomes the only (innocent) suspect.

Locard's exchange principle drives the "expectation" of the investigator that a DNA profile recovered from a crime scene must have something to do with the crime event. On the contrary, it is not a foregone conclusion that a "trace-DNA" profile *will be* recovered from the perpetrator. Donors of background and investigator-mediated contaminant "trace-DNA" will automatically become suspects if the perpetrator is absent from the profile:

The Hidden Perpetrator Effect

Note that a significant proportion of forensic testing is "speculative": areas with no visible body fluid are sampled in the search for evidence. It is commonplace for the perpetrator DNA to be absent from these samples. It is not a foregone conclusion that a perpetrator always leaves a DNA profile at a crime scene. Neither is it true that a visualized DNA profile has anything to do with the crime event. Yet these assumptions are often made. Background, or investigator-mediated contamination, is the biggest risk, previously identified by Gill and Kirkham (2004). If the perpetrator DNA is absent from the crime stain, then the donor of the contaminant DNA becomes a suspect and the perpetrator is hidden (indeed a database search will eliminate him). In addition, a body fluid, such as blood, may be simultaneously detected from an individual using presumptive tests. But there is no assurance that the body fluid and DNA are from the same individual. Consequently, a false association may be made between the contaminating DNA profile and a body fluid detected. "The hidden perpetrator effect" leads to the "association fallacy" where an innocent individual may be implicated in a crime and his DNA wrongly attributed to a body fluid. If this is semen, for example, then it will compound the error further by suggesting the *activity* of sexual assault.

Note the converse will also apply. A perpetrator may have been correctly identified, but his DNA may be absent from the crime scene. DNA from innocent people may be recovered from the crime scene instead. The perpetrator may argue that his absence of a DNA profile and the presence of other unexplained DNA profiles proves his innocence. This sequence of events is quite common in "cold-case reviews" where old cases are reopened for investigation. Here, the miscarriage of justice results in a correctly identified perpetrator being released because of the illogical reasoning explained above.

1.5.3 The Naïve Investigator Effect

I define the tendency for the DNA evidence to override any neutral or exculpatory evidence as the "naïve investigator effect":

The Naïve Investigator Effect

The naïve investigator effect is inspired by the case of wrongful arrest of Adam Scott where a man was arrested, accused of rape and incarcerated on the basis of a DNA-profile match resulting from a contamination incident (Section 2.1). The DNA profile was eventually traced to a contamination incident, but the case is notable because the match was adventitiously obtained from a search of the national DNA database. The exculpatory evidence was initially ignored. To summarize the definition: the naïve investigator finds the closest match to a crime stain in a national DNA database, he ignores exculpatory evidence and seeks to prosecute the matching individual, ignoring other evidence in the case. There doesn't have to be a database search involved—any DNA profile found at a crime scene will do.

1.5.4 Compounded Error Effect

Finally, it is possible to succinctly summarize the cause of "miscarriages of justice." They occur because of the "compounded error effect" that combines the three main effects listed above: the association fallacy; the "hidden perpetrator effect"; and the "naïve investigator effect." False deductive logic driven by "confirmation bias" leads to a cascade effect that propagates multiple errors that address the ultimate issue of guilt/innocence of a defendant:

The Compounded Error Effect

Best illustrated by continuing with the same example: "the wrongful arrest of Adam Scott." Here, a mixture of DNA profiles were recovered from a vaginal swab. One contributor matched the defendant. Other contributions matched the boyfriend and victim, respectively. However, the DNA attributed to *sperm* from Scott was an investigator-mediated contaminant that originated from his *saliva*. Sperm were observed in a vaginal swab but this could be attributed to recent consensual sex with the boyfriend—so *a priori* it was not unexpected to find sperm in the sample. In addition, there was *no* DNA from the perpetrator in the sample (he was absent)—although we can only know this from a proven miscarriage of justice. The investigator begins with "Locard's exchange principle": "every contact leaves a trace" extended to the "expectation," "every perpetrator leaves a trace" and "confirmation bias" drives the interpretation forward, leading to a cascade of errors:

1. The perpetrator DNA was absent. Therefore, the foreign DNA became the only suspect (the hidden perpetrator effect).
2. The presence of sperm was associated with the male profile (from saliva) that came from Adam Scott (the association fallacy).
3. The error was cascaded to falsely deduce that the suspect had had sexual intercourse with the victim—and this addresses the ultimate issue of guilt/innocence (the second association fallacy).
4. Exculpatory evidence—the defendant had alibi evidence that he had never been to Manchester where the rape occurred was dismissed by the investigator—i.e., the "swamping effect" where the one in one billion evidence of the DNA profile overrides all other considerations (see Section 4.17).
5. The investigator has already formed an "expectation" about the guilt of the defendant, and the evidence is literally fitted to the prosecution explanation of the crime—even to the extent that the scientist evaluates, and dismisses the proposition that the defendant has never been to Manchester, despite the fact that this information cannot be deduced from a DNA profile (classic example of "confirmation bias").

Not all errors are captured before going to trial—hence, it is important to analyze and to learn from mistakes. Several cases are analyzed in the book: the death of Meridith Kercher (The Conti-Vecchiotti Report, 2011) and *Regina v. Jama* (Vincent, 2010) (convictions occurred and miscarriages of justice were later identified). Serious "high profile" quality failures are examined in detail: including the Omagh bombing trial (Queen v. Sean Hoey, 2007); "the Phantom of Heilbronn" (Anon., 2009); "death of Gareth Williams" (Anon., 2012b); the "wrongful arrest of Adam Scott" (Rennison, 2012). Two further cases *Regina v. Weller* (2010) and *Regina v. Cleobury* (2012) are also examined in detail. Both cases resulted in convictions and no miscarriages of justice are yet proven.

Although there is a direct relationship between quantity of DNA detected and the chance of a contamination event, the risks cannot be connected to any definition of low-template (or low-copy-number) DNA profiling method (Gill and Buckleton, 2010). All methods are susceptible to some level of contamination. The difficulty is to characterize and to measure the risks so that it becomes an integral part of the court-going statement of the reporting scientist.

This is particularly poignant given that the new multiplexes have been introduced into casework, along with sensitive instrumentation such as the AB3500 (Kirkham et al., 2013), which effectively means that all forensic laboratories are routinely analyzing sub-nanogram DNA samples.

A series of "recommendations" are listed. It is hoped that this will focus widespread discussion and agreement on "best practice" to avoid future miscarriages of justice.

1.6 THE LIKELIHOOD RATIO

See Balding (2005, pp. 22–42) for a review of the likelihood ratio, briefly summarized here.

The likelihood ratio (LR) is the ratio of two probabilities of the Evidence (E) that are evaluated under different hypotheses. The evidence (E) is a DNA profile in this example. The two different alternative hypotheses (propositions) that are evaluated are as follows:

The prosecution hypothesis (Hp): the suspect is the offender.
The defence hypothesis (Hd): an unknown person is the offender.

Note that it is usual for the pairs of propositions to be formulated as opposite alternatives.

The evidence is always conditioned on each hypothesis in turn:

1. There is a DNA profile and it matches the suspect (S) without any ambiguity. This is exactly what the prosecution expect to observe, *if* the DNA evidence has indeed originated from the suspect. Probabilities are strictly conditional, provided there is no "ambiguity" in the profile: $Pr(E|Hp) = 1$. This means that the probability of the evidence if the prosecution hypothesis is true is 1 (i.e., certainty).
2. The defence claim that the DNA evidence is from an unknown person (U)—because the suspect is not the donor of the DNA evidence. In the absence of any error, this can only happen if a random individual has been selected with exactly the same profile as the suspect (this can be refined to include relatives of the suspect).

If there is a full DNA profile recovered, there is a remote probability that it will be observed in a random man—we will use one in one billion, hence $Pr(E|Hd) = 1/1\text{billion}$.

The likelihood ratio is used to quantify which of the two alternative propositions is more likely:

$$LR = \frac{Pr(Evidence|S)}{Pr(Evidence|U)} \qquad (1.1)$$

In the example:

$$LR = \frac{1}{Pr(1/1billion)} \qquad (1.2)$$

hence: LR= 1billion

This evaluation of the evidence is expressed: "the evidence is one billion times more likely *if* the DNA profile originates from Mr S rather than *if* it originates from an unknown, unrelated individual."

An LR > 1 supports the prosecution hypothesis of inclusion, whereas an LR < 1 supports the defence hypothesis of exclusion.

A common mistake is to "transpose the conditional" (the Prosecutor's fallacy); the error is to evaluate $Pr(Hp|E)$ and $Pr(Hd|E)$ instead of $Pr(E|Hp)$ and $Pr(E|Hd)$. The prosecutor's fallacy is committed as a verbal error. For example, the scientist may say: "The probability *that* the DNA profile came from someone other than Mr S is one in one billion." The key to understanding the fallacy is the choice of words—the use of the word "*if*" in the first statement makes the connection between E and H in $Pr(E|H)$ clear, whereas as the word "*that*" implies $(PrH|E)$. For a full discussion, see Evett and Weir (1998, pp. 227–229).

Likelihood ratios can easily be expanded to take account of any set of different hypotheses. For example, a mixture of two individuals may be recovered. The hypotheses to compare may be:

$$LR = \frac{Pr(Evidence|Hp)}{Pr(Evidence|Hd)} \qquad (1.3)$$

$$= \frac{Pr(Evidence|S + U)}{Pr(Evidence|U + U)} \qquad (1.4)$$

Under Hp, the mixture is the suspect and an unknown person, whereas under Hd, it is a mixture of two unknown persons. If the sample is from a known victim (V), e.g., vaginal swab, then it would be standard practice to condition on $Pr(Evidence|Hp) = S + V$ and $Pr(Evidence|Hd) = U + V$; under Hd the suspect is always replaced by an unknown.

1.7 THE ROLE OF THE FORENSIC SCIENTIST

The role of the forensic scientist is to provide an objective assessment of the evidence. Interpretation of evidence within a "framework of propositions" (Cook et al., 1998; Evett et al., 2000, 2002; Gill, 2001) usefully describes the various "levels" at which evidence may be evaluated. The framework provides an hierarchy where the probative value of the evidence increases at each level and is described as follows:

1. The *sub-source* level refers to the strength of evidence of the DNA profile itself.
2. The *source* level refers to an evaluation of strength of evidence if a DNA profile can be associated with a particular body fluid, such as semen or blood.
3. The *activity* level associates the DNA profile with the crime itself, e.g., sexual assault.
4. The highest level deals with the *ultimate issue* of guilt/innocence.

The court has to decide the highest level (guilt/innocence) in order to convict or exonerate a defendant. The information provided by the scientist begins at the lower end of this scale (*sub-source*) and relates solely to the fact of the DNA profile, irrespective of *how* or *when* transfer occurred, and independent of the body fluid origin. The higher the level of the proposition, the more information the court receives from the scientist. The different levels rely on different assumptions to consider and are very case specific. Therefore, strength of evidence estimates will also change significantly as each level is considered (Evett et al., 2002).

The body fluid or cellular origin is an important consideration. For example, the association of a DNA profile with semen automatically implies sexual contact. In an allegation of sexual assault, association of sperm with a given DNA profile is much more probative than confirmation of a DNA profile, without supporting evidence of the body fluid origin.

From the UK legal perspective, the purpose of the scientist is usefully summarized in the Attorney-General's booklet (Guidance Booklet for Experts, 2010) as follows:

When compiling your report/statement you should ensure that due regard is given to information that points away from, as well as towards, the defendant(s).

In Henderson (2010), the court ruling was:

the realistic possibility of an unknown cause must not be overlooked. Where that possibility is realistic, the jury should be reminded of that possibility and instructed that, unless the evidence leads them to exclude any realistic possibility of an unknown cause, they cannot convict

Recommendation 1: The expert should provide the court with an unbiased list of all possible modes of transfer of DNA evidence (Section 5.12).

CHAPTER 2

A Deep Analysis of the Basic Causes of Interpretation Errors

2.1 AN EXEMPLAR CASE: ADAM SCOTT

A recent UK regulator's report (Rennison, 2012) provides a detailed insight into a case where a man was wrongfully arrested and charged with the crime of rape. The errors were identified before a trial could occur.[1] It is important to understand the reasons for the errors and to understand the implicit dangers. For every error discovered, there are an unknown number that are undiscovered.

---

[1] At the same time it must be appreciated that an individual was wrongfully incarcerated for 5 months for an avoidable error.

The circumstances can be summarized as follows: the laboratory analyzed the case using the SGM plus system and obtained a partial (17 allele)[2] DNA profile that was reported with strength of evidence of one in one billion in favor of the prosecution hypothesis. This evidence was sufficient for the prosecution authorities to issue an arrest warrant and the individual was duly charged and incarcerated, pending trial. A contaminated negative control should have rung alarm bells, but it was dismissed without any further action.

Five months later a contamination incident was confirmed by reanalysis of the original swabs and the individual was released. The consequence of the contamination incident was not just confined to a wrongful DNA match, as the error was *compounded* by: (a) misidentification of the body fluid or source of the DNA and (b) wrongful assumptions on the *activity* of sexual assault.

Scientists need to be extremely cautious if an assessment is made that goes beyond the simple fact of a DNA profile match. For example, the DNA statistic calculated for the strength of evidence of the DNA profile cannot simply be transposed to encompass the body fluid of origin and subsequently used to infer the activity that led to deposition. There is always some additional uncertainty to consider beforehand, which will always reduce the combined strength of evidence.

2.1.1 Background to the Contamination Event
New robotics had been installed at the laboratory. Validation studies had been carried out and the data assessed by the UK accreditation bodies NDU (National DNA Database Delivery Unit) and United Kingdom Accreditation Service (UKAS) and permission was duly given for the laboratory to begin processing using the new methodology.

2.1.2 The Crime Events: The First Incident
The first incident was a saliva sample submitted to the laboratory by police as the result of a "spitting incident" by the defendant (a relatively minor offence). The saliva sample was analyzed on 6 October and reported as a "match." The reference DNA profile was uploaded to the national DNA database.

---

[2]Details of the DNA profile have not been released hence the veracity of the strength of evidence cannot be independently verified with this particular case.

2.1.3 The Crime Events: The Second, Unrelated, Incident

The second incident was very serious. A woman was attacked and raped in Manchester on 2nd October, 2010. The exhibits for analysis consisted of two vulval swabs, two low vaginal swabs, two high vaginal swabs. Semen was detected on each of the swabs and separated from other cellular material by differential extractions, each fraction was analyzed for DNA.

2.1.4 Results of the Analysis

The analysis was carried out on 7th October. The low, high, and one vulval swab produced DNA profiles from the seminal fraction, identified as the victim's boyfriend.

The other two vulval swabs gave a mixture from the seminal component containing the victim's boyfriend and an unknown male with 17 alleles present (profile not available for review).

2.1.5 The Contamination Event

On 11th October, it was discovered that a stack of plastic trays removed as waste from one of the robotic units was incorrectly reused. This was reported internally as a quality incident. A number of samples were rerun as a result. The matter was not escalated, and the case which was the subject of the regulator's report was processed on 7th October and was not identified as "at risk" by the processing laboratory.

Recommendation 2:

- If a negative control shows a partial, or full, DNA profile, then this indicates that the batch of samples concurrently processed may be compromised and should be completely rerun.
- There may be implications for the casework procedure in general and the source of the profile should be investigated by comparison with staff elimination databases, the national DNA database (NDNAD), and any other samples processed during a relevant period of time.

The DNA profile was submitted to the NDNAD on 17th October and a "match" with Adam Scott, the defendant, was made. There followed a report written by the forensic scientist which is reproduced in full below (taken directly from the regulator's report; Rennison, 2012):

2.1.6 The Written Statement

Written Statement—Adam Scott

It is estimated that the chance of obtaining matching DNA components if the DNA came from someone else unrelated to Adam Scott is approximately one in one billion (one billion is one thousand million). In my opinion the DNA matching that of Adam Scott has most likely originated from semen.

Interpretation and conclusions:
The DNA detected in the sample recovered from (victim's name) vulval swab (GE2b) can be accounted for by a mixture of DNA from (victim's boyfriend) and Adam Scott. In my opinion these findings are what I would expect if Adam Scott had some form of sexual activity with (victim's name). In order to assess the overall findings in this case I have therefore considered the following propositions:

• Adam Scott had vaginal intercourse with (victim's name)
• Adam Scott has never been to Manchester and does not know (victim's name)

In my opinion, the scientific findings in relation to (victim's name) vulval swab provide strong scientific support for the view that Adam Scott had sexual intercourse with (victim's name) rather than he did not. However, given the position of the semen matching Adam Scott and an absence of semen on (victim's name) internal swabs, the findings do not specifically support vaginal penetration with ejaculation inside the vagina. They may also support vaginal-penile contact with external ejaculation or vaginal intercourse with no internal ejaculation.

2.1.7 Analysis of the Statement

The UK regulator did not comment on the statement itself, but this is critical to understand how errors are compounded within the reporting process itself. It is important to note that two conditioning assumptions are implied by omission, in the statement: *given the position of the semen matching Adam Scott*:

• There was zero chance of a contamination event.
• All of the (male) DNA originated from semen.

Transposition of the likelihood ratio from the *sub-source* level to higher levels of the propositions framework has the effect of *compounding the errors*:

Recall the framework of propositions (Section 1.7). The probability of the evidence if the DNA profile was from a random man is one in one billion. This probability is only conditional upon the fact of the DNA profile, without any assumptions required about the mode of transfer, i.e., the probability is equally valid if the DNA resulted from contamination or if it was transferred as a result of the crime event. The difficulties arise as we address the subsequent levels in the propositions framework.

This is amply illustrated in the statement, where the (same) probability has been associated with a *source*, namely, body fluid (semen) and a verbal statement applied to an *activity*: "sexual assault." The error in the report is that it is not made clear that the levels of uncertainty increase with each level of the proposition addressed. A new statistic is required to incorporate the additional conditional constraints that are implicit with each level of the propositions framework.

Given that the defendant denied any contact with the victim, this kind of reporting also impinges directly upon the ultimate issue of guilt/innocence. A court may be misled into believing that a likelihood ratio is applicable to an *activity* that is closely related to the ultimate issue (as in this case).

To summarize, there are two issues raised:

• The association of the DNA with the body fluid source.
• The association of the DNA profiling evidence with the activity of sexual assault.

If there is any uncertainty about the association of the body fluid with the DNA profile, then the strength of the evidence is always reduced (Aitken and Taroni, 2004; Thompson et al., 2003).

2.1.8 What Are the Alternative Explanations of the Body Fluid Source Evidence?

For any given crime stain, we can generalize two alternative explanations of the source level evidence:

1. The body fluid and the DNA have the same source.
   or
2. A body fluid/tissue has been identified, but the DNA has originated from a different (unidentified) body fluid/tissue.

2.1.8.1 Association of Body Fluid with DNA Profile

The body fluid identification and the DNA profile are *independent* tests that are not equivalent in sensitivity. Peel and Gill (2004) demonstrated that positive presumptive tests for a body fluid (e.g., blood or saliva) could be obtained without a concurrent DNA profile from the depositor, i.e., the body fluid test was more sensitive than the DNA test. Therefore, low levels of body fluid originating from an individual A can be superimposed upon DNA from epithelial cells of individual B (there is no routine test for this tissue) and they can be deposited at different times. The error is that the scientist mistakenly associates the DNA profile from individual B with the body fluid from individual A (where there is insufficient DNA to detect from A). This is another example of the "association fallacy" which is the precursor to the "compounded error effect," illustrated in the case of Adam Scott: his DNA originated from saliva cells but was wrongly attributed to sperm cells which came from a boyfriend of the victim.

Recently, there have been great advances to identify body fluids using RNA analysis. These tests provide much more definitive answers compared to the older presumptive tests, but the same problem emerges in that the association of a body fluid with a "trace-DNA" profile is not implicit. Harteveld et al. (2013) carried out a study on mixtures of DNA and body fluids. The study concluded:

> *Variation in DNA and RNA stability was observed both between and within cell types and depended on the method inducing degradation. Taken together, we discourage to associate cell types and donors from peak heights when performing RNA and DNA profiling.*

Therefore, the implementation of new body fluid identification markers does not alleviate the problem of association of a detected body fluid with a DNA profile—it is not possible to transpose the likelihood ratio applied at the "sub-source" level to the "source" level in the framework of propositions. A different probabilistic model is required at "source-level" in order to calculate the likelihood ratio conditioned on a DNA profile and body fluid if they originate from a single person, compared to the alternative proposition if they originated from different persons. Clearly, much more research is needed in this area in order to provide data that can be used to inform "source-level" inferences.

2.2 THE MISCARRIAGE OF JUSTICE IN R. v. JAMA

There are some remarkable similarities between the case of Adam Scott and the case of R. v. Jama (Vincent, 2010). The latter case was prosecuted in Melbourne, Victoria, Australia, in 2006. Both Scott and Jama had been accused of an unrelated crime shortly before a second more serious incident—in both cases, DNA from the first contaminated the evidence in the second case. By studying the background of R. v. Jama, it is possible to gain valuable insight into the thinking that resulted in the "compounded error effect" that led to the arrest and charging of Scott.

2.2.1 R. v. Jama: The Case Circumstances

Farah Jama was arrested in relation to two unrelated offences committed on consecutive days. Both incidents were alleged rapes. The first victim had been examined in a hospital and samples included vaginal swabs, skin swabs, a portion of hair and clothing was taken for further examination. However, no charges were made against Jama in relation to this alleged offence, and the case was dismissed.

The second victim was examined one day later in the same hospital examination room by the same medical officer. There were four swabs taken from the second victim that were DNA profiled. On one of these swabs there was one intact sperm and 15 sperm-heads observed. The DNA profile matched Farah Jama.

2.2.2 The Second Case Circumstances

The victim had been found unconscious due to intoxication, in a toilet at a nightclub in Doncaster. The toilet was locked from the inside. She had no recollection of events and no recollection of sexual assault. She stated that she had had no recent sexual activity.

The suspect (Jama) denied knowledge of the incident; he said that he had not heard of the nightclub and claimed that he had never been to the Doncaster area at any time.[3] No one had observed him, or anyone fitting his description. Alibi witnesses gave evidence to support his contention that he had been elsewhere at the time of the incident, but this had no positive impact on the jury.

---

[3] Note parallel with Scott.

The police could not find any evidence that Jama had been to the nightclub. There was no fingerprint evidence; no CCTV evidence; no witness evidence; no telephone record evidence. It was considered to be very unlikely that a sexual assault had taken place in the toilet cubicle; if this was true, then the only logical explanation was that the offence must have been committed some distance away and she must have been physically dragged to the cubicle; the offender must have then locked the cubicle from the inside and climbed over it to make good his escape, without attracting any attention in a crowded nightclub.

Police investigators were aware of the first alleged offence and were sufficiently concerned about lack of any other evidence to forward a memorandum to the forensic laboratory:

> ... I need to discount the possibility of cross contamination. Perhaps a report is required.

The response from the laboratory which was considered to be crucial to the subsequent history of the case was:

> In my opinion I do not think contamination between the two cases could have occurred as items from the two cases and the relevant reference samples were examined at different times, at different areas and by different people. Also the DNA processes were done at different times such that the samples were not processed together in the same batch

But this response did not consider the possibility of cross-transfer in the examination room.

In addition, legal representatives for the defence were not made aware that two sets of tested materials were obtained by the same doctor at the same location:

> ... the defence did not challenge any of the prosecutors' assertions concerning the absence of any risk of contamination whatever as they were operating on the same assumptions. The trial judge was not alerted to any problems hence the jury arrived at their verdict on the basis of a fundamental misconception:

At trial, the jury enquired as to whether there were any statistics relating to incidents of contamination. The response was:

> No there was no evidence of contamination in this case

In the final prosecutor's address:

There was no suggestion in this case of any lapse or error, including contamination type error about which the laboratory has got techniques that reveal such a thing if it happens . . .

Note: it was incorrect to suggest that there was a test for contamination and that it could be detected. Indeed, the review (Vincent, 2010, p. 31 of the report) took pains to correct this assertion:

there is no particular test for contamination.

The conviction was eventually quashed as it was established that the DNA profile had transferred via contamination (as outlined in Figure 2.1), although the precise route could not be established—either it occurred at the medical facility but the possibility of transfer within the processing laboratory itself could not be excluded.

In Jama, the errors were compounded by scientists, police investigators, lawyers, and the judge to such an extent that there was manifest failure at all levels of the criminal justice system. Science and Law are supposed to rest on logic, but it seems that the entire legal process can itself by "contaminated" by the "CSI effect" and "confirmation bias" (Section 1.3.9) (http://en.wikipedia.org/wiki/Cognitive_bias#cite_note-26). The official 81 page report (Vincent, 2010) said:

the DNA evidence appears to have been viewed as possessing an almost mystical infallibility that enabled its surroundings to be disregarded. The outcome was, in the circumstances, patently absurd.

To summarize, the cases of Scott and Jama share the following similarities:

1. DNA was located on only one of several swabs taken from the alleged victim.
2. The DNA profiling evidence was "sole-plank."
3. Other evidence, including Alibi-evidence was not considered seriously, because the DNA evidence was weighted above all "other evidence" (or lack of it).
4. The presence of sperm was associated with the DNA profile of the respective suspects (the association fallacy).
5. The presence of sperm was used to infer sexual assault (the association fallacy).

2.2.3 How Did Cross-Contamination Transfer Occur?

In Scott, the transfer mechanism was relatively easy to adduce. This was not the case in Jama. The contamination involved a microscopic amount of material containing his DNA transferred from the first victim to a swab and slide obtained from examination of the second victim. The possibility that it occurred in the hospital was considered to be "quite high" but the conclusion was:

> Precisely how it may have happened cannot be determined as the deposition of the minute amount of material involved could have occurred in a number of ways. It is possible to speculate about the probability of transference through various mechanisms, but ultimately it is pointless to do so.

This advice is pertinent to the on-going court-debate on the "death of Meredith Kercher" (Chapter 5); the original conviction was quashed on similar grounds—the court could not exclude the possibility of DNA transfer via contamination, although the precise routes could not be adduced.

Recommendation 3: The possibility of investigator-mediated contamination outside the laboratory environment cannot be excluded. The laboratory cannot dismiss the possibility by proxy of its own protocols and practice.

2.3 CHARACTERIZATION OF ERROR

The UK regulator's report (Scott) indicated that:

> The error that led to the contamination has occurred on at least two occasions, one identified on 12 October 2011 and again in this case. However, checks against approximately 26,000 samples and the results of their DNA profiling results have identified no further cases of contamination across or between unrelated cases processed from 1 March to 12 October 2011.

There are too few details known to make an assessment of the efficacy of the method used to discover errors. It is probable that pairwise comparisons of all samples in microtiter plates was undertaken in order to determine if there were duplicates appearing between wells.[4] However, for the reasons explained in the Jama case, this process only examines one contamination route out of numerous possible routes, and certainly would not capture all

---

[4]Microtiter plates are typically composed of 96 or more adjacent wells into which DNA samples are pipetted.

potential cross-transfer events. Furthermore, it does not measure the error rate (or probability of error).

2.3.1 Investigator-Mediated Contamination: Definition

Investigator-Mediated Contamination

An investigator-mediated contamination event is the introduction of DNA and/or body fluid that is "external" to the case itself. The introduction is mediated by a third party that may be an investigator at the crime scene, a scientist analyzing the samples in the laboratory, or a manufacturer who has contaminated plasticware (Gill et al., 2010), or a reagent. This is distinct from "background contamination" which describes the presence of DNA that was already part of environment of the crime scene, before the crime event itself occurred.

Contamination (of any kind) can have two different consequences:

- False inclusion where an individual is wrongly implicated
- False exclusion where an individual is wrongly excluded (in conjunction with "hidden perpetrator effect," Section 1.5.2)

An example of an investigator-mediated contamination incident, compounded by a transcription error, leading to wrongful exclusion was reported early in 2012—death of Gareth Williams (the so-called spy in the bag incident) (Anon., 2012b).[5] A contaminating "trace-DNA" profile from an investigating officer should have matched his reference on an elimination database, but failed to do so because a transcription error was made prior to upload. A similar mistake under different circumstances, e.g., a search for a serial rapist could have dire consequences.

The most serious errors tend to be *compounded* and lead to a "cascade effect"—i.e., more than one error is made within a case that effectively leads to misleading results and confusion.

In the Williams case, there was a contamination incident; a transcription error; a failure to match on the national DNA database. Another example of an external contamination error which led to false inclusion of an unknown

---

[5]Note this error could have been very easily avoided simply by an independent check of the DNA profile before upload to the database.

individual is provided by the example of the "Phantom of Heilbronn" (Anon., 2009). Swabs used to collect evidence were contaminated at manufacturing source by a single female individual. This example also shows the "serial error effect" *between* unrelated cases—the "trace-DNA" profile of this (innocent) individual was discovered from more than 40 crime scenes and each time it was wrongly assumed to be the profile of the perpetrator. The "hidden perpetrator effect" is simultaneously demonstrated since they were absent from the crime stain profile. Note that a significant proportion of forensic testing is "speculative"—surfaces with no visible body fluid are sampled in the search for evidence. It is commonplace for the perpetrator DNA to be absent.

2.3.2 Further Exploration of the Contamination Route in Scott and Jama

By studying verified incidents, the route that leads to "false inclusion" via "investigator-mediated contamination" can be generalized in Figure 2.1:

1. Case A is reported, the crime sample DNA is loaded onto the casework NDNAD and the defendant's DNA is simultaneously loaded onto the reference sample NDNAD.
2. Case B crime stain has no DNA from the perpetrator—note that given the extreme sensitivity of DNA testing it is common for crime stains to have no DNA from the perpetrator.

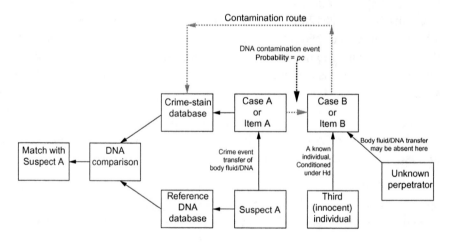

Figure 2.1 Illustration of the transfer route from suspect A to case A and then to case B by contamination. If there is no transfer from the true perpetrator then the "hidden perpetrator effect" (Section 1.5.2) results in DNA from suspect A being visualized that is detected after database trawl.

3. Case A contaminates unrelated case B.
4. A match with the reference sample is declared after the DNA from the crime stain is loaded onto the national DNA database.

2.3.3 DNA Can Transfer Between Items

Figure 2.1 can be further generalized. Instead of "Case A" and "Case B" substitute "Item A" and "Item B," where one item, such as a knife (B), may be evidential, and the other item (A) may be clothing taken from the defendant, such that DNA transfer from the clothing (A) may affect knife (B).

Research by Goray et al. (2012a) showed that the transfer of DNA between packaged items was a distinct possibility:

Overall, this study demonstrates that DNA transfer within packaging is not only a possibility but, under certain conditions, a very likely occurrence.

Relocation of DNA profiles within a single item was demonstrated—for example, if DNA relocates from the handle of a knife to its blade, then this will affect the interpretation of the results.

The authors concluded:

To conclude, the present study demonstrates that while in transit, packaged crime scene exhibits are potentially transferring DNA containing material not only to inside of their packaging, but also to other parts of the exhibit, or even to other exhibits within the same package.

These studies take on extra significance when it is considered that items in cases are often packaged together in large paper bags. There are many imponderable aspects to casework. For old cases, which are reanalyzed years after a crime event, there may be no concise history of item handling, and therefore the significance of findings is compromised from the outset, especially if the following conditions are met:

1. The case is historical and items were collected and stored before DNA profiling was in common use.
2. Evidential items have been packaged together (especially if some items are significant to the offence (e.g., a knife), whereas other items are not).
3. The packaged items may not be properly sealed.
4. Record keeping may be incomplete with limited information of how, when or under what conditions, items have been examined—e.g., if items

are examined/handled consecutively on the same bench then this will provide ample opportunity for cross-transfer.

5. If there are heavily blood-stained items (clothing), then there is very high chance of cross-transfer to other items packaged together.

6. The methods used to detect "trace-DNA" are "ultra-sensitive," detecting a handful of cells.

- *In fact, it would be surprising if cross-contamination had not occurred in cases such as these.*

Another example was the Omagh Bombing trial, where the contamination of evidence was considered to be a real possibility and led to the case being dismissed.[6] Judge Weir said (Queen v. Sean Hoey, 2007):

> it is difficult to avoid some expression of surprise that in an era in which the potential for fibre, if not DNA, contamination was well known to the police such items were so widely and routinely handled with cavalier disregard for their integrity.

It will always be difficult to prove cross-transfer of DNA. There is a perception that such events are uncommon, but absolute truth is always unknown—"what is not known" may have greater impact than "what is known," but the former cannot be presented as factual evidence. This is why the elucidation of error rates, along with new methods to investigate crime scene "background DNA" are urgently needed.

2.3.4 The Burden of Proof: Death of Meredith Kercher

The *possibility* of contamination was central to the initial quashing of convictions in the miscarriage of justice in "Death of Meredith Kercher" (The Conti-Vecchiotti Report, 2011)—although there was debate about the origin of DNA evidence itself, this was secondary to the question of "how did it become evidence."

The storage of items was raised as a significant issue. A knife (item 36) had been packaged in an envelope, then removed at a police station by an individual who had searched the suspect's room some hours earlier, and then transferred it into a nonsterile box. It is impossible to know if contamination did actually occur by this route, but the possibility remains.

---

[6]For example, evidence samples were packaged in bags with holes in them.

A bra-clasp (item 165B) was forcibly removed from the victim during the offence at the crime scene. It was found 46 days after the crime event[7] and upon analysis, a mixture of the victim and defendant (Sollecito) was reported. In conjunction with the evidence of the DNA profiles from the knife (item 36) these findings were central to the original conviction—i.e., the implicit assumption made was that the transfer was associated with the crime event itself.

Subsequent reappraisal of the evidence led to the quashing of the initial conviction on the grounds that the onus of proof that contamination had *not occurred* was clearly the responsibility of the prosecution. The judgment (The Hellman-Zanetti Report, 2011) dismissed the probative value of the DNA evidence as follows:

> In any case, the arguments set forth above, which refute the idea that the burden to prove the source of contamination rests on the defendant making that claim, should be recalled here: it is, on the contrary, those using that result [as evidence] to support an accusation who have to prove that the procedure and, prior to that, the collection stage happened in accordance with the methods and precautions necessary to avoid contamination. As noted above, this did not happen here.
>
> Therefore, the possibility of using the presence of Raffaele Sollecitos genetic profile on the hook of the bra as a reliable piece of circumstantial evidence ceases to exist.

Also recall the statement in the R. v. Jama report that emphasizes the futility of speculation where alternative transfer routes are possible (Section 2.2.3).

An analysis of the Kercher case is outlined in Chapter 5.

Storage and separation of items, and their handling requires significant attention to detail. If there is even a remote possibility that items have been handled inappropriately, then cross-transfer must always be put forward as a realistic explanation, and the crime scene investigation is therefore compromised. The European Network of Forensic Science Institutes (ENFSI) provide best practice manuals (ENFSI, 2008) for investigators to follow. Guidance is not always followed, or a case may be irretrievably compromised because samples were collected and stored before the dangers of cross-contamination were fully appreciated (as in the Omagh Bombing trial).

---

[7]It was of particular concern that the item was discovered a significant period of time after the crime scene investigation started—there was ample opportunity for the item to be moved and contaminated with background DNA.

These studies and case examples take on extra significance in the context of the new multiplexed systems that are now implemented throughout Europe. These new systems demonstrate increased sensitivity to sub-nanogram levels typical of "trace-DNA." In addition, the Applied Biosystems 3500 instrumentation has demonstrable increased sensitivity (Kirkham et al., 2013). This means that DNA profiling is much more powerful and discriminatory, but there is the concurrent increased risk of cross-transfer to consider.

There is a need to extend the work of Goray et al. (2012a). There is also a need to accept that error rates are never zero and much more *pro-active* effort needs to be applied so that the effectiveness of "best practice" can be established and actively measured.

2.4 DETERMINATION OF ERROR RATES

2.4.1 Use of Proficiency Tests

The NRC 1992 report (National Research Council, 1992) recommended:

> *Laboratory error rates must be continually estimated in blind proficiency testing and must be disclosed to juries. For example, suppose the chance of a match due to two persons having the same pattern were 1 in 1 m, but the laboratory had made one error in 500 tests. The jury should be told both results; both facts are relevant to a jury's evaluation.*

The recommendation was reinforced by NRC 1996 (National Research Council, 1996, p. 88).

2.4.1.1 Purpose of Proficiency Tests

Proficiency tests do not directly measure error rates, but are useful as exploratory methods to discover potential weaknesses in analytical processes before they escalate into serious problems.[8] Blind proficiency tests are also needed to compare results between different laboratories in order to ensure that standards are comparable. Most proficiency testing is declared beforehand, but the disadvantage is that the scientist is aware he is under scrutiny and takes special care. Consequently, this does not provide a realis-

---

[8]The author has had personal experience of utility of blind proficiency trials (where the scientist is unaware he is being tested) at the Forensic Science Service. This process was invaluable to coordinate the activities of five separate laboratories to ensure consistency of results and to act as an early warning system. Occasionally, weaknesses were highlighted that led to in depth reviews and corrective actions.

tic assessment of proficiency within the specific pressures of casework. The GEDNAP exercises (Rand et al., 2004) are declared trials used by the majority of European laboratories. There is a useful discussion in Butler (2009, pp. 291–301), who reviews the entire accreditation/proficiency process. Koehler (2010) also recognizes that measurement error is complex and he usefully describes proficiency testing as a "first-pass error rate estimate" and states:

Without such information, legal decision makers have no scientifically meaningful way of thinking about the risk of false identification and false non-identification associated with forensic reports.

In Jama, at trial there was a firm rebuttal of any possibility of error in this (specific) case which sounded very convincing, but was based solely on "what *we think* we know to be true." The problem is that knowledge of the circumstances of a case is always incomplete. If an error has happened, it will not be obvious, and cannot be evaluated by advocacy. It will usually be impossible to identify when or how it happened and this is why a *generalized* error rate is needed to counter-balance the imponderable uncertainties that are inherent to any prosecution case.

2.4.2 Principles of Risk Management When There Is Contamination to Consider

How can useful generalized error rates be adduced? Gill and Kirkham (2004) carried out an extensive study on the impact of contamination in a typical forensic casework environment.[9] They analyzed real casework results and associated negative controls in order to make a generalized assessment of the risks that were associated with contamination. For practical reasons, the experimental design could only consider within laboratory contamination, but it could be extended to the evidence recovery stage by submitting "blank" samples at the same time as crime stain samples. The general conclusions were:

1. No process is free of contamination.
2. There is no test for a contaminant profile (cannot be distinguished from any other profile).
3. Contaminants tend to be quantitatively low level.
4. Contamination rates can be characterized by reference to negative controls.

---

[9]This is the only published study that has attempted to estimate contamination rates in a caseworking environment.

5. The greatest risk was identified as the "hidden-perpetrator" effect (Section 1.5.2).[10]

In respect of point (4), negative control monitoring can be carried out in order to assess the general "health" of a routine analytical process. This is in addition to the utility of the negative control that is used to indicate a problem *within* the processed batch of samples, along with the relevant negative control. In casework it is not possible to identify *which* samples are contaminated—only the probabilities can be estimated.

Gill and Kirkham (2004) carried out a detailed analysis that showed that a description of contamination is complex, as it is dependent upon several factors. Gross contamination incidents tended to be low level and are often in admixture with a "relevant" profile (i.e., a profile that is evidential). There is nothing implicit in the DNA profile that provides information to decide whether it is or it is not a contaminant. From a simulation of 14,750 mixtures, based on real casework from the FSS, the authors showed that there was a probability of 0.001 that a match probability $< 10^{-7}$ would be reported from an external contamination source, given a reporting limit of detection threshold of 50 rfu. The most likely contaminant sources were investigators, laboratory staff, and contamination of plasticware (Gill et al., 2010). All three are partly addressed by utilization of investigator and manufacturer databases. The primary risk was identified as "adventitious," i.e., chance matches of a "crime stain" DNA profile to the national DNA database—where the risk of matching was increased because the partial nature of the DNA profile itself; the adventitious match probability can be subdivided into two categories:

1. *The random man adventitious match*
   The probability of a chance match between two unrelated people, where one is discovered by trawling a database, has been widely discussed in the literature, e.g., Aitken and Taroni (2004). See Chapter 4 for a full discussion.
2. *The same man adventitious match*
   For the UK national DNA database, there is a 60% chance that a submitted crime stain will "match" an individual (Bramley, B. In: Fraser and Williams, 2009, pp. 309–337). This is because, a large proportion of the offending male population is already present on the national

[10]Where investigator-mediated or background contamination occurred and the perpetrator is not a contributor to the recovered DNA profile.

DNA database—therefore, the high chance of a match is driven by recidivism (because offenders tend to be serial) and the resultant matches are not "random man adventitious," because the DNA originates from the *correctly identified individual* so we can define this event as a "same-man-adventitious-match."

The "same-man-adventitious-match" is independent of the match probability of the genotype. If a suspect has been concurrently identified with a case (A) then his profile is automatically placed on the NDNAD. If DNA from case (A) is inadvertently transferred to an unrelated case (B), then an adventitious match is almost certain to occur. The chance of "same-man-adventitious-match" is dependent upon the gross contamination rate probability (p_c) within the analytic process and it follows that for a full DNA profile:

$$p_c >> p_m$$

The 1992 NRC recommendation (National Research Council, 1992) to report the error rate from proficiency testing concurrent with the *random-man* chance match statistic to the courts is compelling. Ideally, a summary is needed of statistical errors that flow as a consequence of a contamination event. In particular, we need to discover:

1. The probability of a false exclusion
2. The probability of a false inclusion

There is no reason why results of proficiency exercises and negative control logs should not be compiled and made available for inspection by courts as a matter of routine (recall that there was a specific jury request in the case of Jama). Such information would be useful to assist courts to place strength of evidence calculations into perspective and may be crucial for the jury to consider, if the "other evidence" in the case is not compelling.

The first step is to estimate general contamination rates, and to begin to partition the probabilities according to the various ways that transfer is known to occur. Modes of same-man-adventitious-contamination (within the analytical process) can be subdivided as follows (this is an incomplete list):

1. Transfer via used plasticware
2. Aerosol transfer between samples
3. Sample mislabeling or loading samples into the wrong tube

Therefore p_c is composed of at least three probabilities—further subdivisions are possible. In the Scott case, some *post hoc* effort was made to identify potential contamination incidents (details have not been released). Although it is possible to estimate contamination rates, it is not possible to identify *which* profiles are resulting from contamination incidents. Although *post hoc* analysis is useful to detect obvious examples of contamination, it will not detect all cases within the family of errors, and therefore cannot be used to retrospectively adjust the error rate—for every error detected, there will certainly be an unknown number that remain undetected.

2.5 REPORTING DNA PROFILES AT SUB-SOURCE LEVEL

A priori, the scientist has no information about whether the interpreted profile is relevant to the case. Interpretation proceeds by formulation of alternative hypotheses, or propositions, to reflect the beliefs of the prosecution (Hp) and the defence (Hd). Recall the "framework of propositions" (Section 1.7). There are several hierarchical levels, the first described as "sub-source" is the lowest level, since it just considers the fact of the DNA profile itself, without considering any other information in the case. The two alternatives considered are:

- The DNA profile came from the suspect (Hp)
- The DNA profile came from an unknown (unrelated) person (Hd)

It is noteworthy that the analysis is conditioned purely on the fact of the DNA profile without any consideration of the circumstances, hence as a raw probabilistic analysis, it is always correct, even if the source of the DNA is from contamination.

2.5.1 Limitations of DNA Evidence and the Use of Caveats

Recall the UK Attorney General's advice (Guidance Booklet for Experts, 2010):

> When compiling your report/statement you should ensure that due regard is given to any information that points away from, as well as towards, the defendant(s)

Gill (2001) advised that caveats should be used in relation to *sub-source* level reporting (statement of limitations, Section 1.2.1)

2.6 REPORTING DNA PROFILES AT SOURCE LEVEL

2.6.1 Transposing the Likelihood Ratio to the Source-Level: The Association Fallacy

It is common practice for forensic scientists to attempt to place some further meaning on the DNA profile. In particular, courts are usually interested in the "source" of the DNA profile—can it be associated with a body fluid? In the Scott case, the allegation was one of sexual assault, hence the question arises whether the DNA profile can be *associated* with sperm.

Association of DNA with a body fluid is often assumed—then the probability of the DNA evidence is simply transposed to the body-fluid. In the case of Scott reviewed here, the contamination error was compounded by the resultant statement to the court, where the reporting scientist said:

> *It is estimated that the chance of obtaining matching DNA components if the DNA came from someone else unrelated to Adam Scott is approximately one in one billion (one billion is one thousand million). In my opinion the DNA matching that of Adam Scott has most likely originated from semen.*

Here, we observe the phrase "most likely," replaced later in the statement by: "given the position of the semen matching Adam Scott." The scientist may consider it possible to rank the possibility of semen above other cell types, such as skin, but this is not a probabilistic argument, merely one of subjective contention. Its juxtaposition to the statement "one in one billion" gives the impression that the statistic could be applied directly to the presence of semen. The error is primarily one of omission, since alternative methods of propagating the evidence are not discussed, i.e., the statement was not fully inclusive of *all possibilities*, including those that cast doubt on the prosecution argument. This effectively limits the court to a consideration of the single possibility that was mentioned—which was semen. There was no caveat to mention that the strength of the evidence would be limited by the contamination rate. This may not be intuitive to a court, and therefore needs to be actively introduced into the proceedings so that it may be properly considered.[11]

---

[11] It will be argued that the preferential extraction method should provide the necessary confidence, but this is undermined by the contamination rate; the fact of the partial low-level profile; and the lack of demonstrable reproducibility of replicate analyses of the stains analyzed.

The problem is amply illustrated by the fact that DNA from Scott did *not* come from semen—it came from saliva. Semen attributed to the perpetrator originated from the victim's boyfriend. This was common ground under both the defence and prosecution hypotheses. Finally, the "hidden perpetrator effect" (Section 1.5.2) meant that the contaminating profile was the only possibility available to connect with the crime event (the perpetrator was effectively eliminated). Therefore, the error of the DNA contamination incident was *compounded* by transposition of the likelihood ratio, applied to the DNA evidence, to its source—worse, this automatically implied activity of rape (and the ultimate issue).

There is very little in the literature on the association of the DNA evidence with the body fluid source (Harteveld et al., 2013; Peel and Gill, 2004). The starting position is the *sub-source* level calculation of the strength of evidence. Doubtless, the greater the quantity of body fluid recovered, the greater the confidence that an association can be made, but currently this relationship cannot be quantified. This is clearly an important topic of discussion for the forensic community to address. In a review by Jackson, G. In: Fraser and Williams (2009, pp. 419–446) the practice of transposing the likelihood ratio is discussed:

> *Provided that semen had been identified on the vaginal swabs; the profile obtained from the preferential extract from the swabs gave a single, male profile of appropriate strength; it is accepted that the woman had had no previous sexual contact with a man for many weeks; then it seems reasonable to assign a probability of approaching 1. If this is so then the LR for the "source" level will be of the same magnitude as the "sub-source" LR.*

In the Scott case, the principle "no sexual contact for many weeks" was transgressed—therefore, the association was inappropriately made if this criterion is followed. In Jama, the "victim" had had no recent sexual contact, and this certainly contributed to the allegation of rape, but as we have seen, the inference was wrong. The presence of semen on a vaginal swab does not by itself prove an allegation of rape. The cases under discussion provide a dramatic illustration of how contamination caused false association that led directly to the ultimate issue of guilt/innocence. The "association fallacy" is the precursor to miscarriages of justice and therefore seems to be much more dangerous than the better known "prosecutors fallacy" (Aitken and Taroni, 2004).

Recommendation 4: If a body fluid is identified from a known contributor, this information cannot be used to hypothesize the body fluid origin of any additional contributor in a mixture of body fluids/tissues.

In summary, the association of a DNA profile with the body fluid is never implicit and it is incorrect to simply assign the strength of evidence of the DNA profile to imply the *association of the DNA profile with a body fluid*. The assessment of DNA evidence is underpinned by sound genetic theory that enables very small match probabilities to be elucidated but no such theory exists for the assignment of the probability of the association of the body fluid and this is driven largely by presumptive tests and "expert opinion." In a review by Aitken and Taroni (2004, p. 425) where the effect of error is similarly explored, it is also concluded:

> *Extremely small match probabilities can therefore be misleading unless the relevant error probabilities are also extremely small.*

The *source* and *sub-source* probabilities cannot be transposed.

2.6.2 Inferring Source from DNA Quantity: The Case of R. v. Weller

This case (*Regina v. Weller*, 2010) is interesting since contact between the victim and defendant was not denied. There would be some prior expectation that DNA transfer would occur between the two. However, in this case digital penetration was alleged and therefore the inference was that vaginal cells were present underneath the defendant's fingernails. The inference was made solely on the basis that the relatively high quantity of DNA attributed to the victim was more likely to be present if digital penetration had occurred rather than nonsexual contact.

2.6.2.1 The Case Circumstances

The victim and the defendant met at a party, the victim drank steadily and became violently ill, vomiting in the bathroom. The defendant took her to her bedroom and she alleged that he sexually assaulted her by digital penetration. A pathologist confirmed injuries were present that were consistent with the allegation. The defendant denied the allegation and stated that:

1. he helped her to bed,
2. he pulled hair out of her eyes to stop her vomiting on it,
3. he picked up her clothes,
4. he placed the alleged victim in the recovery position.

Following a complaint to police, fingernails were clipped from the defendant from both hands. The nails were swabbed and DNA profiles obtained. The left hand revealed a mixed profile that matched the defendant along with a minor (full profile) that matched the victim, and the right hand revealed a profile only from the defendant. There was no dispute that the minor component of the DNA profile was from the alleged victim. Therefore, the only point of contention was the body fluid source of the victim's DNA.

2.6.2.2 Ranking the Possibilities
In court, the possibilities were enumerated as follows:

1. Contact with hair of the victim.
2. Touching the victim when putting her into bed or holding her in the recovery position.
3. Contact with vomit from the victim.
4. Insertion of fingers into the vagina of the victim.
5. Secondary transfer from the victim's clothing which the defendant picked up.

Note that transfer methods (1–3) and (5) are the alternative innocent explanations, whereas (4) was the offence route.

2.6.2.3 Evaluation of the Evidence
The court-debate concerned a non-probabilistic discussion about the likeliest mode of transfer. Published papers were used to inform the debate. The transfer of DNA to fingernails is well researched, but simultaneously illustrates the difficulties of extracting meaningful probabilities from publications, which can be used in real casework.

The starting point is to discover the background prevalence of foreign DNA under fingernails. This is relatively low: In a study by Cook and Dixon (2007), it was observed that only 6% of samples produced DNA mixtures; Cerri et al. (2009) obtained 5% of samples producing mixtures—when couples were monitored, it was observed mixture ratios varied between 20:1 and 1:1 (Malsom et al., 2009)—these levels did not appear to be related to the amount of time spent together or the time interval between sexual contact (if any) and sampling, i.e., we can generalize that there is low probability of transfer under general circumstances.

Conversely, controlled experiments by Flanagan and McAlister (2011) showed that there was very high probability of vaginal cells being transferred to fingernails as a result of digital penetration.

This information was sufficient to convict Weller of the offence. However, there was no attempt made in court to carry out a probabilistic analysis, hence, the approach used at trial was intuitive.

From the published observations, the key features of the experimental evidence can be summarized here as:

- (Hp—prosecution): There is a very high probability of DNA transfer if digital penetration occurs Pr ≈ 1.0.
- (Hd—defence): There is a low probability of DNA transfer if digital penetration has not occurred (one of the methods enumerated above resulted in DNA transfer) Pr ≈ 0.06.

In the absence of a test for vaginal cells, the likelihood ratio is formed as follows:

$$LR = \frac{Pr(E|Hp)}{Pr(E|Hd)} \tag{2.1}$$

where E is the evidence of the DNA profile, Hp is the prosecution hypothesis that DNA was transferred by digital penetration, and Hd is the defence hypothesis that DNA was transferred by one of the innocent methods enumerated above.

Hence, the LR $= 1/0.06 = 16.6$

Under this rationale, the evidence is 16 times more likely if it originated from digital penetration than if it originated via some innocent source. There could be argument about the value of $Pr(E \mid Hd)$ but given the experimental data on background profiles, it is unlikely to be lower than 0.01. A reasonable range for the LR would be: 16.6–100.

The analysis here is over-simplistic, since one important potential source of the DNA: the victim's vomit, was dismissed at trial. The data do not exist on this type of evidence to carry out a similar analysis to that just described—an example where absence of evidence is not evidence of absence.

The case is interesting since the source of the DNA was inferred solely by its presence and the circumstances of the case—there was no attempt to evaluate if vaginal cells were actually present. If a logical approach is followed, the strength of evidence used for conviction was weak, if calculated in LR terms, and was many orders of magnitude lower than that required for a DNA profile to be considered probative.

Allegations of digital penetration or sexual assault are quite common. It is worth emphasizing that there was no dispute about the contact between

Weller and the alleged victim, therefore the observation of the DNA profile on fingernails of Weller has limited relevance since it could be explained by several alternative transfer methods including contact with the victim's vomit. Conversely, given that Weller denied any recent sexual contact, a confirmatory test to detect the presence of vaginal cells would have been highly relevant to the case—and much more probative than the DNA evidence. Recent tests developed by the Netherlands Forensic Institute (NFI) using RNA analysis (Lindenbergh et al., 2013) include a confirmatory test for vaginal cells, and this offers a level of objectivity that cannot be matched by quantitative assessment of a DNA profile.

Conclusion:

- Strength of evidence to infer body fluid source in R. v. Weller was much lower than for classical DNA analysis.
- Inferences obtained by quantification of DNA profiles are speculative.
- Detection of body fluids using RNA methods provide the basis of an objective method to test for vaginal cells.

2.7 ACTIVITY LEVEL REPORTING

It is remarkable in the Scott case that the laboratory "compounded" the errors further by considering in great detail, the *activity* that led to the presence of the DNA profile. Consider the statement that follows:

> *In order to assess the overall findings in this case I have therefore considered the following propositions: (a) Adam Scott had vaginal intercourse with (victim's name) (b) Adam Scott has never been to Manchester and does not know (victim's name).*
>
> *In my opinion, the scientific findings in relation to (victim's name) vulval swab provide strong scientific support for the view that Adam Scott had sexual intercourse with (victim's name) rather than he did not. However, given the position of the semen matching Adam Scott and an absence of semen on (victim's name) internal swabs, the findings do not specifically support vaginal penetration with ejaculation inside the vagina. They may also support vaginal-penile contact with external ejaculation or vaginal intercourse with no internal ejaculation.*

The phrase "strong scientific support" is used without qualification in the statement, but is equivalent to 1 in 10,000, according to Buckleton et al. (2004). The level of support was a purely subjective view—there was no rationale presented to support such a statement. No conditioning was presented and no formal probabilistic assessment was given.

2.7.1 Further Analysis of the Conditioning (Activity) Statements Used in Scott

The idea behind the probabilistic assessment is to mirror probabilistic arguments using language rather than mathematical formalization. This typically involves choice of "opposite hypotheses," e.g., the suspect under the prosecution hypothesis is replaced by a random unknown person under the defence hypothesis.

Note that the alternatives evaluated in Scott were:

- Adam Scott had vaginal intercourse with (victim's name).
- Adam Scott has never been to Manchester and does not know (victim's name).

But there is no way to tell from a DNA profile if someone has visited Manchester. The problem with this arrangement is that there are effectively three different sets of hypotheses combined together. In a proper analysis, these sets of hypotheses would be expressed and evaluated as follows:

Set A:

- Adam Scott had vaginal intercourse with (victim's name).
- Adam Scott did not have vaginal intercourse with (victim's name).

Set B:

- Adam Scott has been to Manchester.
- Adam Scott has never been to Manchester.

Set C:

- Adam Scott does know (victim's name).
- Adam Scott does not know (victim's name).

With set B the reporting scientist clearly had insufficient prior information to determine whether the defendant had or had not been to Manchester and it seems to have been presented as personal opinion. Indeed the veracity of the defence argument was later confirmed by mobile telephone records that showed that the defendant had not been in Manchester at the time the offence was committed. This is a classic example of "confirmation bias" where the investigator conveniently negates defence arguments that do not fit the "expectations" of the prosecution.

Set C propositions were irrelevant, since it was common ground that the defendant did not know the victim's name.

Recommendation 5: To formulate sets of alternative hypotheses, they must be logically constructed, so that the alternatives mirror each other. Different hypotheses must never be combined together (unless supported by formal probabilistic analysis).

2.7.2 Inferred "Activity" from a Partial DNA Profile Without Source Evidence: *Regina v. Cleobury* (2012)

In R. v. Cleobury, the only evidence was a mixed and partial DNA profile (alleged victim to defendant transfer) obtained from the defendants boxer-shorts. There was no transfer of DNA alleged to have occurred from defendant to victim. The DNA evidence on the boxer-shorts was used to infer the activity of sexual assault (without any supporting evidence of body fluid). Cleobury was convicted of rape and the conviction was upheld after appeal.

2.7.2.1 Case Circumstances

The defendant (Cleobury) and the alleged victim (V) were at a party. The defendant had recent sexual intercourse with his girlfriend (G). V alleged that she had been raped by Cleobury at the party, although no ejaculation took place. V also had consensual sex with her boyfriend previous to the incident. She was examined 10 h afterwards. No DNA profile that could be attributed to Cleobury was detected on vaginal swabs or her knickers. No sperm were detected.

Cleobury was examined 13 h after the incident, penile swabs were taken and his boxer shorts were analyzed for DNA. The DNA profile from a penile swab was entirely attributable to a mixture of Cleobury and his girl friend (G). *A priori*, since both defendant and victim had both engaged in consensual sexual activity with their respective partners, evidence of vaginal fluid/sperm transfer would have had no significant impact on the interpretation of the evidence as their respective origins could not be ascertained.

2.7.2.2 The Boxer Shorts Evidence

The central, front portion of the underpants yielded a complex DNA profile (no semen detected). The profile was reported as originating from at least three individuals. The prosecution report reads:

In my opinion, V can be considered a potential contributor of some of this DNA, albeit at low level.

The statement follows:

Cleobury Statement

If it is accepted that V's DNA is present on Mr Cleobury's underpants, then given the accounts of the two individuals concerned, I can consider the following two propositions:

- Mr Cleobury had vaginal intercourse with V
- Mr Cleobury did not have vaginal intercourse with V and did not have any sexual or physical contact with her

In my opinion, the findings provide moderate support for the first proposition rather than the second.

2.7.3 Analysis of the Statement
2.7.3.1 The Alternative Defence and Prosecution Hypotheses

To formalize, the prosecution proposition (Hp) contended that the profile was explained as a mixture of Cleobury, G and V, whereas the defence proposition (Hd) explained the profile as a mixture of Cleobury, G and an unknown person(s) (not V). The person of interest (POI) is the person who donated the DNA profile. Under Hp the POI is the victim since the alleged transfer is from the victim to the defendant; under Hd the transfer is from an unknown person (not the victim). The likelihood ratio formulation is:

$$LR = \frac{\Pr(E \mid \text{Cleobury, G, V, Hp})}{\Pr(E \mid \text{Cleobury, G, U, Hd})}$$

When the propositions are formulated in this way, it would be the normal procedure to calculate the strength of evidence in probabilistic terms where a number is used to impart the strength of the evidence. The outcome of this analysis may favor the prosecution hypothesis of inclusion of the person of interest (V), or it may favor the defence hypothesis of exclusion. In this case, there was no probabilistic analysis that was carried out by any of the forensic scientists; hence the strength of scientific evidence was not adduced.

It is clear that the prosecution case can be described as follows:

- There was a major component attributed to G (Cleobury's girlfriend).
- There were additional minor components that could be attributed to Mr. Cleobury.

- There were two alleles that could not be attributed to G or Mr Cleobury: the prosecution contended that these were present in the victim's (V) profile.

In her report, the prosecution scientist stated:

> *The vast majority (18 out of 20) of V's DNA components were represented in this result. Therefore in my opinion, V can be considered a potential contributor of some of the DNA in this result.*

It is well established that significant sharing of alleles will occur between unrelated contributors of mixtures (Buckleton et al., 2007; Paoletti et al., 2005). Therefore, from the defence perspective, the relevant question to ask is: *if the person of interest is not V, how likely is it that 18 out of 20 components will match* (I will address this issue later in Section 2.7.4). The prosecution scientist then proceeded to address the activity that could have led to the presence of a DNA profile from V, stating:

if it is accepted that V's DNA was present[12]—two alternatives were considered:

- Cleobury had sexual intercourse with V
- Cleobury did not have sexual intercourse or physical contact with V

Note the violation of recommendation 5: as with Scott (Section 2.1) the formulation of the alternative hypotheses are muddled and are another example of prosecution-anchored "confirmation" bias. Recall that the alternative propositions must be balanced. The defence proposition in this case simultaneously evaluates two different alternative methods of transfer: namely, sexual intercourse *or* physical contact, whereas the prosecution proposition only considers the activity of sexual intercourse. To be valid, the following constructs would be needed:

Set A:

- Cleobury had sexual intercourse with V
- Cleobury did not have sexual intercourse with V

---

[12]Note that the jury accepted the premise because the defendant was found guilty. However, the jury was invited to speculate without any probabilistic assessment of the evidence by the scientist. It is easy to see how "confirmation bias" takes over in the absence of sufficient guidance by the "expert" scientist.

Set B:

- Cleobury had physical contact with V
- Cleobury did not have physical contact with V

These distinctions are necessary since under the prosecution hypothesis Set A addresses a criminal offence, whereas Set B does not.

The prosecution scientist finally formed the conclusion:

the scientific findings provide moderate support for the first proposition (of sexual intercourse). Moderate support is equivalent to 1 in 100 (see Buckleton et al., 2004, p. 40). There were no scientific data to inform this statistic, however.

2.7.4 The Relevance of the Matching Components
The defence scientist noted that one component did not reach the required standard for reporting; this means that there were 17 out of 20 matching alleles. The defence question now becomes: how likely is it that 17 out of 20 alleles match if a mixture of three (or four) persons are compared with a random individual? To evaluate this hypothesis, computer simulation can usefully provide an answer as follows:

- Generate four DNA profiles labeled i, ii, iii, and iv.
- Generate a mixture by combining profiles i, ii, iii (simulating defendant, girlfriend (G), and a random, unknown person (U); this forms the basis of the defence hypothesis).
- The fourth profile (iv) is victim V under the prosecution hypothesis. Under the defence hypothesis it is *not* V, rather it is an unknown person (Note that V is simulated as a random genotype).
- Record the number of alleles that match the fourth profile, by chance.
- Repeat the above steps one thousand times to generate 1000 numbers representing the distribution of the number of alleles that match by chance.
- The results of the analysis are shown in Figure 2.2.

The analysis demonstrated that approximately 4.5% of observations had 17 or more matching components, with a maximum of 19 matching components observed. The prosecution scientist stated that the mixture comprised three or more individuals, hence it was relevant to carry out an additional assessment under the assumption that there were four contributors to the mixture, namely: the defendant, G, two unknown individuals (Figure 2.3).

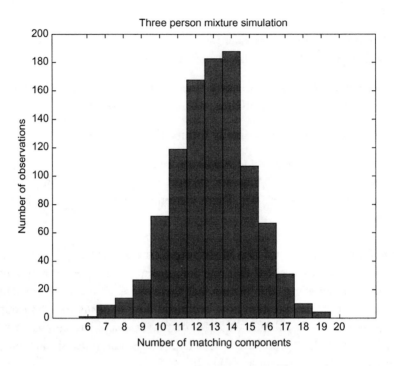

Figure 2.2 Three person mixture compared to a random individual (1000 simulations), showing the distribution of matching components when compared to a random individual.

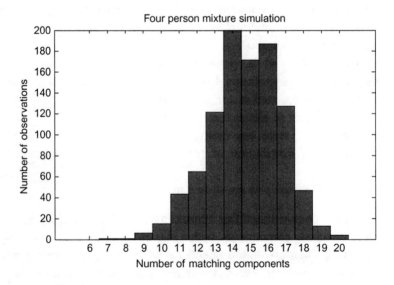

Figure 2.3 Four person mixture compared to a random individual (1000 simulations), showing the distribution of matching components when compared to a random individual.

This analysis showed that there was a very high, 20% chance, that 17 or more components will match a randomly chosen individual. Furthermore there were four observations (out of 1000 total) where all 20 components matched a random man.

An approximate likelihood ratio can be constructed:

- Hp: The chance that V will match 17 or more alleles in stain, given that she has contributed.
- Hd: The chance that a random person will match 17 or more alleles in a mixture of four individuals.

To summarize, the evidence is 5 times more likely if the prosecution proposition is true than if the defence proposition is true.

In Chapter 4 there is further discussion on the matching allele count method applied to partial profiles. It is shown that generalizations from the "full" DNA profile to partial (degraded) DNA profile are not possible. Also it is shown that courts can be persuaded by "experts" to endorse procedures that have no scientific basis.

2.7.5 The Debate on Secondary Transfer
Given that the DNA evidence was weak, the following court debate on secondary transfer was not particularly relevant but is included as a demonstration of "compounded error" effect.

First, the jury was asked to speculate in the absence of probabilistic evidence:

if the DNA came from V. Since a conviction occurred, the jury must have accepted the premise.

Second, the prosecution scientist was asked if it was possible that DNA from V could be transferred to the boxer-shorts via a towel:

it is quite possible that numerous people could have wiped their hands on the towel.

In the absence of data to support the proposition, an appropriate response would be to accept the possibility without ranking it (the answer given seems to evade this important point).

If the towel was believed relevant to the investigation, then the correct response would be to undertake DNA analysis to verify presence/absence of potential contributors—this was not carried out.

2.7.6 Conclusion

1. The only evidence was a DNA profile on some boxer-shorts. The DNA evidence was not considered in respect of the "statement of limitations." Furthermore, comments were not restricted to *sub-source* as the scientist speculated at the *activity* level—effectively addressing the ultimate issue of guilt/innocence.
2. The jury was unwittingly invited to engage in confirmation bias, since it was also asked to speculate *if the DNA came from V* without scientific guidance to support the proposition: in the final analysis, the inescapable conclusions are that there was no meaningful probabilistic evidence: (a) to associate the DNA profile with the victim and (b) to associate the mode of transfer of the DNA profile to the boxer-shorts of Cleobury. It was therefore an error to speculate on the activity that caused the transfer of the DNA evidence that was solely conditioned on the prosecution assumption about the origin of the DNA profile.

Recommendation 6: Assessments of the probative value of DNA evidence from any crime stain where two or more individuals are in admixture requires formal probabilistic analysis, rather than counting the number of alleles that match a suspect. The counting method can be very misleading (Section 4.32).

2.8 THE ROLE OF THE PROSECUTION AUTHORITIES

In the UK, the decision to prosecute an individual is taken by the Crown Prosecution Service. There has to be a realistic chance of successful prosecution beforehand. Doubtless, the decision in relation to Scott was taken as a result of the forensic "evidence"; a statement was provided by the scientist, that relied upon transposition of the strength of evidence of the DNA profile, applied to higher levels within the "framework of propositions." The activity of rape was associated with the DNA profile itself. It does raise serious questions about how common it is for individuals to be prosecuted solely on the evidence of a DNA profile within the UK and elsewhere, and also how widespread is the practice of the false association fallacy by transposition of the LR to imply an "activity" that erroneously leads to the ultimate issue of guilt/innocence?[13]

2.9 THE ROLE OF THE ACCREDITATION/REGULATORY AUTHORITIES

The laboratory that reported the "Scott" case was fully accredited—but accreditation does not prevent serious errors from occurring. This is because the primary focus is on evaluation of written protocols and procedures,rather then pro-active proficiency testing (Section 2.4). It does not necessarily mean that the laboratory actually follows written procedures.

In his report, the UK regulator stated:

I am satisfied that there are no further cases of contamination during the automated DNA extraction process in use since March to 12 October 2011.

The assessment was based on a search for contamination incidents that were open to discovery—presumably by a search for duplicated profiles in unrelated cases. However, Gill and Kirkham (2004) show that most contamination incidents are not duplicated, they are "one-off" events and they are therefore hidden and cannot be discovered. We can assign probabilities that any given DNA profile is a result of a contamination incident, provided that the necessary work is carried out. By way of example only, a generalized assessment by Gill and Kirkham (2004) showed that the contamination rate from a Forensic Science Service (FSS) procedure to be of the order of 1 in 1000. It would be expected to find at least 20 contamination incidents within a batch of 26,000 "affected samples," but it would not be possible to show which samples were affected. A contamination incident often has no effect on a case, other than to reduce strength of evidence—but when "the hidden perpetrator effect" occurs the consequence may be problematic (Section 1.5.2). The contamination rate will vary according to laboratory

---

[13] It is interesting that there is a debate currently taking place in the Scottish jurisdiction on the requirement for corroborative evidence. The argument is that the requirement for corroboration limits the number of successful convictions. However, this clearly places the forensic scientist in a very difficult position, as we have seen that the DNA evidence cannot be properly evaluated, and put into context, unless there is some other significant evidence in a case.

and process used in the analysis, but the rates are unknown unless pro-active assessment is carried out using the methods suggested.,

2.10 THE DATABASE TRAWL PROBLEM

Several authors have commented that the strength of evidence calculation by frequency estimation is unaffected by identification of a suspect by database trawl. Indeed, Balding and Donnelly (1996) show that in a population of N people in a database, the fact that $N - 1$ are eliminated from an inquiry actually increases the strength of evidence.

However, no previous author has considered the effect of recidivism (the same man random match) combined with internal contamination which were the proven causes of the miscarriage of justice in Jama and the wrongful arrest of Scott. In both cases, a database trawl was used to identify the suspects. In both cases, statistics were applied that were based on the frequency of a profile in a population ca. one in one billion.

The classic frequency-based calculation does not consider the contamination effect. An implicit assumption is made that there is no possibility of an internal contamination incident.

1. As databases become very large, for example, UK five million, this means that a very high proportion of the criminal population are already captured on this database.
2. There is a 60% chance that an individual will be identified from a crime stain because of recidivism (UK National DNA Database, 2013) .
3. The probability of an investigator-mediated contamination event is much greater than the chance of a random match.
4. A legal issue compounds the error further in the adversarial UK system of justice—it will never be revealed to a jury that the suspect was identified by database trawl since it will imply previous activities or convictions that would be unfairly prejudicial to the defendant.[14]
5. This ultimately leads to a paradox where the full facts of a case are never revealed to the jury—a statistical strength of evidence is applied that ignores the contamination effect and is not in context of the fact of the database search.

---

[14]This is not an issue for the majority of European jurisdictions working with Inquisitorial systems.

2.10.1 Contamination and the Hidden Perpetrator

When speculative searches are carried out at crime scenes (especially those that sample "invisible" crime stains), it is commonplace that no DNA is recovered. If an investigator-mediated contamination event occurs in combination with the hidden perpetrator effect, then only visible profile is the contaminant itself which has been transferred by "passive" (innocent) means. The donor becomes a suspect since it may be assumed that the transfer was "active," associated with the crime event. An example is the "Phantom of Heilbronn" (Anon., 2009).

The risks can be evaluated as follows: there are two parameters: h is the probability that the perpetrator has *not* contributed to the profile (the hidden perpetrator) and c is the probability of an investigator-mediated contamination. The corresponding events are designated as H and C respectively. In the "Phantom" example, the swabs were contaminated at manufacturing source. In the Scott case, the contamination was from within the laboratory environment—with the latter case, once the contamination had occurred a match on the national DNA database was guaranteed.

Assume a single contributor profile is observed and its probability of a chance match with a random person is very small in relation to $\Pr(C)$. A suspect that matches the crime-stain profile has been identified (by database trawl in the previous example). The prosecution argues that there is no contamination and the perpetrator is the only visible profile, hence the probability is $\Pr(\bar{H}) \times \Pr(\bar{C}) = (1 - h) \times (1 - c)$.

The defence argue that the true perpetrator is *not* visualized and a contamination event *has* occurred with combined probability $h \times c$.

The likelihood ratio is:

$$LR \approx \frac{\Pr(E \mid \bar{H}, \bar{C}, \text{Hp})}{\Pr(E \mid H, C, \text{Hd})}$$

$$LR \approx \frac{(1 - h)(1 - c)}{hc}$$

In Figure 2.4 $\Pr(H)$ takes a value $h = 0.01, 0.1$, or 0.5 to reflect increasing probability of the "hidden perpetrator." When $h = 0.5$, $LR \approx 1/c$. It is clear that the probability of contamination will always be higher than the random match probability of a full DNA profile. It follows that an LR based on contamination risks should be routinely calculated in conjunction with the usual LR statistic that is conditioned on the population

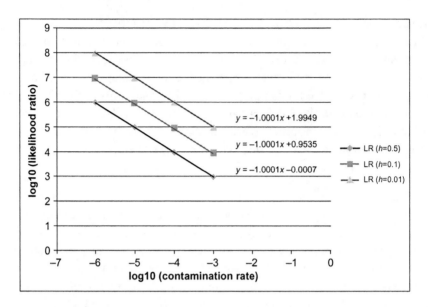

*Figure 2.4 Plot of Pr(C) vs LR=[(1-*h*)(1-c)]/*hc *relative to increasing probability of the hidden perpetrator Pr(*H*) where* h=0.01, 0.1, *and* 0.5, *respectively. When* h=0.5, LR ≈ 1 / c.

frequency estimate. See Section 4.24 for an expanded discussion on the effect of contamination on DNA profiling statistics.

2.11 THE LESSONS OF HISTORY

Errors resulting from investigator-mediated and background contamination events cannot all be discovered *post hoc*. Most are hidden. It may take several decades to resolve errors that involve serious miscarriages of justice. In the UK during the 1970s a string of wrongful convictions related to terrorist offences occurred. Known as the Birmingham six, Judith Ward, the Maguire seven, the Guildford four.

All of the original prosecutions were successful on the basis of positive scientific tests for explosives, where scientists expressed their opinions on the strength of the evidence associated with the activity of handling explosives, illustrating the *compounded error* effect. An excellent summary of events is provided by Schurr (2012).

Here, the problems of the scientific evidence were related to the error of omission—i.e., a failure to explain to the court that materials, other than explosives could cause a false positive. The compounded error was provided by "expert-opinion" from impressive prosecution experts with years of experience. Although defence scientists expressed misgivings, their evidence was not taken seriously by the court who deferred to the greater "experience" of the prosecution expert. Later it was found that kits used in the testing were contaminated. There were also examples of negative control results being ignored.

Is a parallel theme emerging with DNA analysis? In the UK a recent court ruling *Regina v. Weller* (2010) effectively gave a "green light" to expert opinion, unsupported by probabilistic assessment, where a body fluid was adduced from quantity of DNA alone (the probabilistic assessment carried out here suggests "weak" strength of evidence). In Scott the results of a negative control that indicated investigator-mediated contamination was dismissed. Fortunately the error in Scott was captured before going to trial, but when considered in the context of R. v. Jama, it demonstrates how miscarriages of justice can easily be propagated via all of the "actors" in the criminal justice system.

2.12 THE ESSENTIALS OF STATEMENT WRITING

From a global perspective, there are two schools of thought about how DNA profiles should be reported to courts and this is dependent upon "local" practice and the requirements of the relevant jurisdiction. There are two extremes: either the DNA is reported "as it is" without any further information, or it is reported with embellishment to take account of "likely" sources and activities that led to deposition. Both approaches have problems associated with them. First, a raw statistic is easily misinterpreted by an uneducated court who is likely to be influenced by confirmation bias and equates a matching DNA profile with "guilt." At the other extreme, there are many examples in this book that shows the scientist him/herself to be subconsciously affected by "confirmation bias." The DNA statistic is embellished and effectively directs the court down a narrow channel that usually (if not always) favors the prosecution. This is typified by the statement in Scott (Section 2.1) where the scientist wrongly evaluates the chance of the defendant having visited Manchester.

The challenges can be summarized as follows:
- How can the scientist prepare a balanced statement that is designed to educate a court to think about all possibilities?
- How can court statements be generated that take into account all of the "known information," as well as the "unknown information" that may point towards the innocence of a defendant.

Taken in the context of the framework of propositions (Section 1.7), a generalized statement format is suggested that could have been used in the case of Scott. The key to statement writing is to avoid confusing the probabilities of the DNA evidence with its source and potential mode of transfer (the activity); to avoid the error of omission and the "association fallacy" by stating all possibilities; to ensure that the unknown events are suggested for consideration to a jury; to ensure that the *limitations* of the evidence are recognized. The starting position is that the possibilities are equally weighted. Whether it is valid for a scientist to propose whether one possibility should be favored in relation to another, by ranking, depends upon whether experimental (peer reviewed) evidence is available. Otherwise this would be inappropriate—note that this advice contradicts the court ruling of *Regina v. Weller* (2010) that places "experience" above the requirement of peer review:

> It therefore seems to us that what this appeal demonstrates is that if one tries to question science purely by reference to published papers and without the practical day-to-day experience upon which others have reached a judgment, that attack is likely to fail, as it did in this case.

However, opinions that are not rooted in scientific principles which can be tested experimentally, can only be speculation. Practical day-to-day experience is not a substitute for experimentation under controlled conditions. Conversely, in *Regina v. Reed, Reed and Garmson* (2009), the dangers of the "association fallacy" are recognized:

> There is, we accept, always a danger that if an expert expresses one part of his scientific evidence with confidence, and also expresses other views, those other views can, unless care is taken, be given a verisimilitude of certainty by association.

The issue of association of cellular type with the "trace-DNA" profile was also considered by the Reed judgment:

> the type of cellular material from which it has been obtained is unknown (as was the case here) an expert can in many cases, give evidence enumerating the possibilities.

Hence the advice of R. v. Reed is certainly in keeping with principles outlines in this book, whereas the advice in R. Weller appears to be contradictory.

A discussion on the need to properly structure a statement follows.

2.12.1 Part I: The DNA Profiling Evidence

The core statement is straightforward and follows traditional guidelines (a commentary is provided in italic script):

The statement begins:

I have considered two alternative propositions:

- The DNA profile came from the suspect (Hp)
- The DNA profile came from an unknown (unrelated) person (Hd)

The evidence is one billion times more likely if the former proposition is true.

Note: The reporting scientist now needs to reinforce the point that this probability cannot be transposed to a consideration of the source of the DNA profile:

The expression of the strength of the evidence relates solely to the fact of the DNA profile and it cannot be used to evaluate the source of the DNA profile or the activity that led to the evidence.

There are several explanations for the transfer of the evidence of the DNA profile. Without ranking, these are as listed as follows:

1. The DNA profile was transferred during the crime event
2. The DNA profile was transferred before the crime event (innocent transfer)
3. The DNA profile was the result of a contamination event (inadvertent transfer within the laboratory)

Note: it is incumbent upon scientists to explain all the possible transfer methods, regardless of how unlikely it may be perceived to be. If the court is not informed of the various possibilities, then the error of omission is committed

2.12.1.1 Declaration of Laboratory Contamination Rate

In this laboratory, the contamination rate adduced from a study of negative controls was estimated to be 1 in 1000 samples (for example).

More information could be provided here—in particular the compilation of negative controls should be disclosed along with the results of proficiency tests, with emphasis on "blind trials."

Recommendation 7: If analyses are replicated and/or several stains are analyzed, this is an excellent way to reduce the impact of contamination rates. In Scott only one stain out of five tested showed his DNA profile and this is characteristic of contamination. In Jama, the result was not replicated since only one swab in 4 showed a DNA profile, but this advice will not apply if the item itself is grossly contaminated.

2.12.2 Part II: An Assessment of the Body Fluid Source
Each case will require separate consideration. There is nothing implicit in the DNA profile that indicates its cellular source. The key to reporting body fluids is to report separately from the DNA evidence. The misassociation of body fluid with the "trace-DNA" profile is particularly prone to cognitive bias effects.

2.12.2.1 Cognitive Bias
Although it is possible to describe the various alternatives that could have occurred, the difficulty with real casework is informing the probabilities (e.g., Evett et al., 2002). The variables can be listed, but their probabilities are usually unknown. Consequently, it is all too easy for the expert to misrepresent personal beliefs as scientific principles. This phenomenon is part of known family of cognitive biases. The "mind projection fallacy" is defined by Jaynes (1991) as: *someone's subjective judgments are "projected" onto the real world, rather than being related to personal perception.* This fallacy is committed by the scientist and compounded by elevating a subjective (personal) opinion to be a generalized "scientific principle" (where in fact none exists). A second form of the fallacy is when someone assumes that their own lack of knowledge about a phenomenon (which is a fact about their state of mind) means that the phenomenon cannot be understood. This thinking is typical in relation to "error-rates." A common cognitive bias in forensic science is to assume that a phenomenon that is not understood or poorly researched is believed not to occur or to be irrelevant (but this is a state of mind derived from incomplete knowledge—it does not reflect the real world). Consequently, the lack of scientific evidence to support a phenomenon is often used to reinforce "confirmation bias."

In the Scott case, semen had already been observed in the crime stain. However, this was explained by recent sexual intercourse with the victim's boyfriend. This formed the major component of the DNA profile, and the defendant formed the minor part of the DNA profile. The minor component was partial. It was implicit that observations could be accounted for by a mixture of body fluids.

The alternative (viable) defence hypothesis (that the DNA profile did not come from semen) was never properly evaluated—therefore the error was one of omission—failure to consider *all possibilities*.

The DNA profile and the observation of sperm are two separate facts. It is possible for DNA profiles to be obtained from unrecognized (or untested) sources such as skin cells. Alternatively, the observation of sperm heads does not necessarily imply that the DNA has originated from them (the use of preferential extraction did not provide the necessary assurance in this case).

Recommendation 8: The strength of evidence of a "trace-DNA" profile is always assessed at the sub-source level and this cannot be transposed to the source-level to imply that the DNA is from a particular body fluid (the uncertainty of the association will require a different statistic to be calculated).

2.12.3 Suggested Statement Proforma to Attribute Body Fluid

The following statement is adapted from a suggestion used in a successful appeal in the case of Kerby (2011), where there was uncertainty in relation to the origin of the DNA source. In the original court going statement the reporting scientist had associated the DNA profile with spermatozoa. There was a positive presumptive acid phosphatase test, but few sperm heads had been visualized. On appeal it was accepted that the DNA could have originated from an alternative source (and sperm was one of these sources). At retrial the statement was adjusted to reflect the possibilities. The statement that follows was introduced by the defence and it could be adapted for general use:

I have considered the origin of the cells that gave rise to the DNA profile. The DNA profile is always the same regardless of the origin of the cells. It is not known which cell types are associated with the main DNA profile. It is not known when the cells were deposited. It is possible that the (main) DNA profile could have originated from sperm, an unidentified body fluid, or a mixture of body fluids. It is currently not possible to carry out a statistical assessment of these three possible alternatives. Consequently, it is important to emphasize that the likelihood ratio calculation provided in the statement is not conditioned on the presence or absence of any particular kind of body fluid.

The various cell types that are observed are simply stated, without speculating which specifically gave rise to the DNA profile.

Note: Of course the calculation of combined strength of evidence of the DNA profile with the body fluid is difficult to undertake and there is no example in the literature. An improved understanding of contamination rates, and a deeper understanding of false positives and false negatives is generally needed.

In practice, the fact of the DNA profile and body fluid considerations are best kept separate.

2.13 SUMMARY

As the forensic community continues to process samples with increased sensitivity, this has the undesirable effect of increasing the uncertainty of the association of the DNA profile with the crime event, along with complications of deciding the source of the stain. Background and investigator-mediated contamination are real risks to interpretation. Whereas this has been recognized as a serious issue for several years (Gill and Kirkham, 2004; Gill et al., 2010), to date the implications have not been properly addressed by the forensic community.

Note that contamination does not necessarily lead to misinterpretation since the impact is case-specific. If the contamination occurs when there has been no transfer from the perpetrator, then the "hidden perpetrator effect" can lead to the "false inclusion error" identified by database trawl. It is also possible that a true perpetrator may be wrongly eliminated, if he is not present on the national DNA database, and in admixture with an "internal" contaminant. Then the "association fallacy" leads to the strength of evidence directly applied to higher levels of the "framework of propositions"—namely, the body fluid source. The "compounded error effect" means that several errors are cascaded within the case—the activity of sexual assault was inferred in the case of Adam Scott.

The "serial error effect" shows how errors are propagated across unrelated cases. The classic example is the "Phantom of Heilbronn." Again this error is a consequence of the "hidden perpetrator effect"; there is a belief that the contamination event is linked to the true perpetrator, no matter how unlikely it appears.

All the above errors are in turn symptomatic of cognitive errors such as "confirmation bias" and the "mind projection fallacy" (also known collectively as the CSI effect; Anon., 2012a) where subjective views are projected onto the real world under the guise of "expert opinion." Prosecuting authorities, courts, and others can also be infected (typified by the case of Jama, Section 2.2.1), and this provides a reason why miscarriages of justice occur.

Future work with graphical models or Bayes Nets (Aitken and Taroni, 2004; Biedermann and Taroni, 2012) could be used to explain "all possibilities" to a court without "filtering information" by selectively ignoring hypotheses. The relevant probabilities to use will prove difficult to estimate as every case is different.

CHAPTER 3

A Framework to Interpret "Trace-DNA" Evidence Transfer

There has been significant research on the significance of DNA profiles that are found underneath fingernails. The example discussed in Section 2.6.2 was unusual in that the case-relevant question was not related to persistence of DNA after deposition. However, a typical fingernail-case involves violent assault of a victim who scratches the assailant in self-defense. The victim may be killed during the attack. It is routine for fingernails to be taken for analysis, as DNA found underneath fingernails may reveal a foreign DNA profile that originated from the perpetrator.

It is possible to generalize: if a foreign DNA profile is recovered that matches an individual, then the question inevitably centers on whether the transfer is associated with the assault, or whether there is an innocent explanation. If the suspect denies ever having had any contact with the victim, then the possibilities are limited to (a) transfer during the assault and (b) investigator-mediated contamination.

However, it is common that the defendant has had some previous social contact with the victim. The interpretation of the evidence then has to take into account (a) innocent cross-transfer as a result of innocent contact between suspect and victim and (b) persistence of DNA underneath fingernails. The interpretation of the evidence is dependent upon the timing of the last social contact before the crime event—will the DNA persist underneath fingernails after a given period of time?

As there has been extensive experimental research carried out, the example provides a useful example for a model court report. The following compilation is not based on a specific case but is presented as a fair way to report DNA profiling trace evidence that is demonstrably objective and free of "confirmation bias." All possibilities are actively evaluated by reference to the peer-reviewed literature.

There are two primary objectives for the reporting scientist to fulfil:

• To present an account that incorporates all possibilities that may explain how and when evidence may have been transferred, without bias.
• To ensure that any viewpoint expressed by the scientist is firmly based on the experimental evidence, thereby reducing subjective opinion to a minimum. The aim is to distance the reporting officer from expressing an opinion that is based upon subjective thoughts that cannot be verified or independently tested.

An example statement structure is provided below and relates to DNA profiling evidence taken from fingernail clippings. A commentary is included (readers may wish to incorporate parts of the commentaries into their own statements).

3.1 THE STATEMENT STRUCTURE

Commentary: The first part of the statement is purely factual; it describes the case circumstances and addresses the relevant questions to consider.

1. *Information and purpose:*
   The victim (Ms V) was attacked and died of stab wounds following a night out with friends. During postmortem, a number of biological samples were recovered and fingernail clippings were taken from the left hand. In the context of this case, it is logical to consider if Ms V had had direct contact with her assailant resulting in a transfer of a sample

of their DNA to her fingernails which could then be detected by a DNA profiling test?

2. *Background of Mr S:*
Mr S is the suspect in the case. He was a former boyfriend of Ms V. Mr S stated that he had social contact with Ms V 7 days previously, but none since then.

Commentary: The circumstances of the case have been described. The case-preassesment addresses the expected persistence of DNA over a 7-day period. DNA profiling is carried out and the strength of the DNA evidence is calculated.

3. *The results of the testing:*
The DNA profile mixture produced from an extract prepared from the fingernail could be separated into one major component and one minor component. The minor component profile within the mixture matched the DNA profile of Ms V herself. This result was not unexpected given the origin of the sample tested and is explained by cellular material/DNA from Ms V being present in the prepared extract. The major component profile matched the DNA profile of Mr S. It was calculated that the chance of obtaining the major component profile, if it had originated from someone other than and unrelated to Mr S is approximately one in one million.

Commentary: At this stage of the testing, the evidence has been evaluated without any reference or consideration about how or when the DNA profiles were transferred.

4. *The meaning of the DNA evidence:*
The wording used to describe the statistic is very specific. It is a measure of strength of evidence related to the fact of the DNA profile itself—nothing can be implied regarding how or when the DNA was transferred. The evaluation of the evidence relating to the mode of transfer (when and how) is considered separately as an independent exercise.

Commentary: This paragraph is necessary to alert the court to the fact that the strength of the DNA evidence only relates to the identity of the DNA profile itself. The statistic does not provide any indication about how or when the DNA profile originated, neither is there any information about the kinds of cells that may have contributed the DNA profiling evidence. The statement is purely restricted to factual evidence that is easily tested by the defense expert by referring directly to the raw DNA profiling data, independent of the circumstances that resulted in transfer. Different experts using the same software, and trained in similar ways should reach similar conclusions on the strength of the DNA evidence.

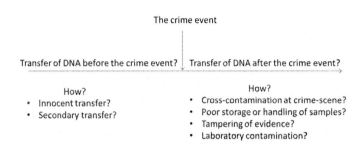

Figure 3.1 A generalized time line showing how evidence may transfer.

5. A statement of the possibilities:
Commentary: Having evaluated the strength of the DNA evidence, we now evaluate how and when the transfer occurred.

A generalized time line can be used to show the various possible methods of transfer (Figure 3.1).

Commentary: Any case circumstance can be fitted to the generalized time line. Usually, the prosecution contend that the DNA transfer occurred concurrently with the crime event itself. The alternative defense hypotheses comprises mutually exclusive parts: (a) either: the DNA is not from Mr S, rather it is from another unknown person[1] *(b) or: if it is from Mr S, then the transfer occurred at some time previous to, or after, the crime event itself. In the example case described here, the defense position is clear in that Mr S visited Ms V 7 days previous to the crime event (Mr S claims this to be his last contact with Ms V).*

The alternative modes of transfer are shown in Figure 3.2.

Transfer of DNA *after* the crime event is also a possibility to consider: a contamination event at the analyzing laboratory would be an explanation. Assuming this to be a remote possibility,[2] the primary consideration that remains is: *if the defense scenario is true, then is it possible that DNA from Mr S may transfer to Ms V after casual contact, and persist underneath her fingernails for a period of 7 days?*

---

[1] This probability is the chance that the matching DNA profile originates from a random man.
[2] The chance of contamination can be properly addressed by the scientist by reference to quality control data from the lab (how many times has contamination actually been observed in the laboratory)?

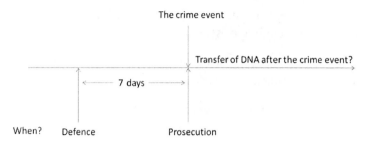

Figure 3.2 Defense vs. prosecution propositions relating to transfer of evidence.

3.2 WHEN AND HOW DID THE "FOREIGN" DNA TRANSFER TO UNDERNEATH THE VICTIM'S FINGERNAILS?

The following framework provides a structure to evaluate when and how the DNA may have been transferred. Recall the defense proposition that the opportunity for "passive" transfer occurred 7 days previously, whereas the prosecution contended that the transfer was "active," a result of the victim scratching her assailant at the time of the offence. The alternative propositions are as follows:

3.2.1 Alternative Propositions Under the Prosecution Hypothesis

(i) The DNA profile recovered from the fingernail (and matching Mr S) had been deposited at or around the time of Ms V's death as a result of direct contact between the two individuals, e.g., by scratching him.
Or

3.2.2 Alternative Propositions Under the Defense Hypothesis

(iia) that the DNA, if it had originated from Mr S,[3] had been transferred to the fingernail as a result of a direct contact between them 7 days earlier
Or
(iib) had been transferred by a secondary transfer mechanism from Ms S touching a surface that had retained Mr S's DNA as a result of his previous presence at her home while in a relationship with her.
Or

---

[3] Noting that the defense do not accept that the DNA was from Mr S in the first place, but was a random chance match with an unknown person.

(iic) Post-crime-event transfer occurred as a result of laboratory contamination or mishandling of samples.

Commentary: Note that this assessment can be provided directly by laboratory data to include negative control compilations.

3.2.2.1 Research and Data Relevant to the Case

Expert opinion is underpinned by experimental data:

Commentary: The various alternative modes of transfer were described in the previous section. This section shows how an expert can be an expert. He/she describes experiments that have been carried out in order to support any opinion that may be used to describe the likelihood of the various alternatives listed. First the levels of background contamination are addressed.

1. *Occurrence of foreign DNA in a random population of individuals*: Before an interpretation can proceed, it is necessary to establish the "baseline." An assertion that the presence of a foreign trace-sample is probative can only be properly assessed if it is known how often foreign DNA will be observed from control samples, i.e., fingernails of random individuals who carry out normal activities. It may well be that these baseline levels will vary according to an individual's occupation and social circumstances (e.g., cohabiting or living alone).

2. *Persistence of foreign DNA*: If foreign DNA is introduced underneath fingernails, how long will it last before it can no longer be detected?

3. *Nature of the DNA profile*: What kind of DNA profile is expected if a given set of circumstances has occurred? *In this case, the relevant scenarios are scratching vs. "passive" transfer.* What are the expectations that the foreign DNA profile will be in admixture with the victim's profile, and will it be a major or minor component of the mixture? How is the expected outcome affected by the persistence of foreign DNA relative to the time of deposition?

Commentary: The prosecution claimed the DNA profile was from the suspect, that transfer was coincident with the assault. The defense argued that the deposition of DNA, if it was from the suspect, occurred 7 days previous to the allegation of assault and there was no further contact between suspect and victim. Are there data that support the notion that DNA will persist underneath someone's fingernails for this period of time? Is it possible that "passive indirect" transfer could occur in the intervening period in the absence of the suspect? Recall that "expectations" can be used to reinforce "confirmation bias," hence this effect is mitigated by the following analysis of the experimental data to underpin "expert-opinion."

Each of the expectations is evaluated directly from the published data as follows.

3.3 BASE LEVELS OF FOREIGN DNA TRANSFER FROM EXPERIMENTAL STUDIES

One of the first studies to contribute to this area was provided by the Environmental Science and Research (ESR) forensic science laboratory in New Zealand (Henderson et al., 2004). They reported that in their pool of test subjects the total incidence of foreign DNA detected in fingernail scraping samples was 8% (4/48 cases) and they concluded that the low incidence of foreign DNA detected under the fingernails of participants in their study suggested it to be unlikely that an individual would have foreign DNA under their fingernails as a result of their normal daily activities.

Corroboration of this observation was also reported by Cook and Dixon (2007). The purpose of this UK study was to assess the background levels of foreign DNA under the fingernails of individuals from the general population who had been together in a social environment. Fingernail swabs from 100 individuals were processed. Foreign DNA was detected in 13% of samples with only 6% of these samples generating reportable mixed DNA profile results. It was concluded that the incidence of foreign DNA underneath the fingernails was low and when detected, the majority were represented at such a low level that they could not be reliably reported. In Matte et al. (2012), results generated from the fingernails of 178 individuals in the general population were examined. Only 19% of these samples contained a foreign DNA source out of which 65% produced poor quality, low-level DNA profiles.

In 2009 further research explored the expectation that if two people cohabited, then there would be a greater opportunity for DNA transfer from the partner to the donor's fingernails as a result of habitual or intimate contact which might account for some of the foreign DNA profiles observed in previous studies. The prevalence of mixed DNA profiles in fingernail samples taken from couples who cohabit using autosomal and Y-chromosome short tandem repeats (STRs) (Malsom et al., 2009).

The incidence of foreign DNA was studied in 12 couples that cohabit. While foreign DNA was detected in 17% of the samples (24/144 cases), most of the foreign DNA detected matched the donor's cohabiting partner, rather than someone else, inferring that intimate contact was required for transfer to occur. These data also accorded with the observations of Henderson et al. (2004).

In summary, this research and data demonstrate that the incidence of foreign DNA beneath the fingernails in the general population as a result of casual social contact is low. Even if the foreign DNA is detected, then invariably this profile can be sourced to a person's partner rather than to a random individual and foreign profiles tend to be at a low level.

3.4 WILL A DNA PROFILE THAT IS TRANSFERRED BY EITHER "PASSIVE" OR PHYSICAL MEANS (SCRATCHING) PERSIST FOR 7 DAYS?

3.4.1 The Experimental Evidence

In the study by Matte et al. (2012), a total of 265 casework samples were examined where scratching had occurred or was suspected to have occurred. The results from the donor fingernails showed increase prevalence of foreign DNA compared to a control set of 178 samples taken from a general population (33% compared to 19%). This supports the inference that scratching promotes the transfer of foreign DNA to fingernails.

The study was complemented by controlled experiments where a participant was lightly scratched (sample size of 10 people) and a second parallel study where participants were scratched more aggressively (sample size of 20 people). Two sets of results were collated: one set immediately after scratching showed that 37% of individuals had a foreign DNA profile underneath their fingernails from which the person that they had scratched could not be excluded as the source. Note that the figure of 37% compares well with the "real casework" set reported, providing confidence that the levels of expectation of transfer are realistic. However, only 17% were reportable profiles.

More vigorous scratching (the second set of experiments) produced better quality DNA profiles (30% were reportable quality), demonstrating that more than casual/light scratching is required for fingernails to acquire and to retain high quantities of foreign DNA. If blood is detected under fingernails, then this increases the chance of detecting the donor: there is the added information on the presence of blood underneath fingernails that may infer violent defensive response from the victim. This may be corroborated by the presence of scratch marks on the skin of the defendant.

3.5 PERSISTENCE OF A DNA PROFILE TRANSFERRED TO FINGERNAILS 7 DAYS PRIOR TO ITS RECOVERY

If the question raised by the defense relates to specific question of persistence of a DNA profile underneath fingernails for a period of 7 days or more, it can be generalized that the profile will steadily erode, for example, as a result of personal washing/bathing habits, it will become partial, and will therefore become low level over a period of time in admixture with the victim's DNA profile. Indeed Matte et al. (2012) demonstrated that after a 7-h delay in collection, only 7% of samples taken had retained foreign DNA (recall that this figure was 37% when samples were taken immediately after the event). Loss of DNA is promoted during daily activities (e.g., handwashing). Clearly if the victim is dead, then the foreign DNA profile would not decay.

The data summarized in Table 3.1 are based on relatively few observations, but provide an insight into the properties of DNA transfer to underneath fingernails. Foreign DNA will be observed in a proportion of the population. If individuals have close contact with each other (e.g., cohabiting couples), this increases the chance of foreign DNA transfer. The chance of "passive" DNA transfer for cohabiting couples is the same as the chance of transfer by an "active" process of scratching. The latter is more likely to provide a probative profile that can be interpreted, however, and certainly the presence of blood underneath fingernails in conjunction with a major foreign component must be a significant finding. Otherwise, the mere presence of a foreign DNA profile does not directly imply scratching, the transfer could also occur by "passive" means.

There is rapid decay of foreign DNA, however, after 6 h, assailant foreign DNA profiles were detected in 7% of experimental victims, and most were too low level to report.

There are lack of data that suggest when DNA has completely dissipated after experimental introduction, termed here the extinction point. We can infer this to be ca. 24 h from hand-holding experiments of Lowe et al. (2002).

Table 3.1 Summary of Experimental Findings

| Author | Method of transfer | | | | |
| | Passive (background) | | Immediate sampling | Active (scratching) | |
	Total (%)	Reportable profile (%)		Immediate sampling	6-h delay
Henderson	8%	?	Total	Reportable Profile	
Cook and Dixon	13%	6%			
Matte	19%	7%	33% (casework)	21%	
Matte			37% (vigorous scratching controls)	30% (vigorous scratching)	7% (all scratching groups)
Matson	37% (cohabiting)	17%			

The background prevalence of foreign DNA underneath fingernails is between 8% and 19%, but only 6–7% are reportable profiles > 5 STRs. When couples cohabit, the prevalence of foreign DNA from a partner is much greater (37%) with 17% reportable profiles. When there is "active" transfer (e.g., scratching), the chance of transfer is much higher (37% for vigorous scratching experiments with 30% providing a reportable profile). After 6 h, the chance of observing a mixed profile drops to 7%.

3.6 CONVERTING POSSIBILITIES INTO BROAD PROBABILISTIC RANGES: A MODEL FOR REPORTING OFFICERS

The data provided above cannot be directly converted into *precise* probabilities, but it is reasonable to support broad probabilistic ranges summarized in tabular form: we can potentially assign subjective probability ranges based on symmetric quantiles, where *very low* is described by $Pr < 5\%$; *low* describes $Pr = 5–25\%$; *medium* describes $Pr = 25–75\%$; *high* describes $Pr = 75–95\%$; very high describes 95–100%. The wide choice of ranges reflects the uncertainty inherent in the data sets (Table 3.1). It is possible that as more data become available that the ranges may be reduced. Conversely, there is no reason why categories cannot be combined, e.g., *low/very low* would encompass a much wider range of uncertainty, $Pr = 0–25\%$. As a specific example, from Table 3.1, experimental data describing the baseline, i.e., chance of "passive" transfer is recorded as $Pr = 6–7\%$, which translates to a low probability, whereas the chance of transfer via vigorous scratching is recorded as $Pr = 30\%$ (medium probability). The data are summarized in Table 3.2.

Commentary: The use of strict conditioning does not preclude the possibility that there had been recent casual or intimate contact between victim and suspect. The role of the scientist is (a) to make the court aware of the possibilities and (b) to act in a passive way, without prejudicing those possibilities that should be considered. There is the clear implication that the court must be an active driver of the discussions that take place, and the role of the expert scientist is very much to facilitate these discussions. By continual reference to evidence of data, the scientist avoids subjectivity and at the same time the court is less likely to be misled. Access to the raw

Table 3.2 A Summary of Expectations, Assigned in Broad Probabilistic Ranges from the Experimental Results from Table 3.1

Chance of a given proposition	Type of transfer	
	Passive	Active
Chance of observing a reportable foreign profile in a random individual (the base line)	Low	
Chance of observing a reportable DNA profile where a donor is a cohabitee	Low	
Chance of transfer of a reportable DNA profile via vigorous scratching (<1 h)		Medium
Chance of observing a reportable DNA profile >6 h after last contact	Low	Low
Chance of observing a reportable DNA profile >24 h after last contact (extinction point)	Very low	Very low
Very low is less than 5%; low describes Pr = 5–25%; medium describes Pr = 25–75%.		

experimental data will itself provide a means to demonstrate the potential
likelihood of trace transfers for given sets of conditions.

However, lack of relevant experimentation will be a common hindrance
to make this kind of assessment for other types of evidence.

3.6.1 The Final Statement/Conclusion
3.6.1.1 Part I: The Strength of the DNA Evidence

1. A DNA mixture was obtained from fingernail scrapings of Ms V. This
   mixture comprised a major profile that matched the reference profile of
   Mr S and a minor profile from Ms V. I have considered two different
   alternatives: either the major profile originated from Mr S or it originated
   from an unknown unrelated person. In my opinion, the strength of the
   evidence is one million times more likely if it originated from Mr S.

3.6.1.2 Part II: The Mode of Transfer of the Major Contributor to the DNA Profile

2. The strength of the evidence of the DNA profile does not impart any
   information about how or when the profile was transferred. The mode of
   transfer, and its timing is a separate consideration. The possible identity
   of the major profile is considered as a separate issue in part I.

3. To formulate my opinion on transfer of the major contributor, I have
   referred to the published literature. There are two alternative explanations
   that are put forward by the prosecution and the defense, respectively:

   • The prosecution contend that "active" transfer of the major DNA
     profile to underneath the fingernails of Ms V was coincident with the
     attack that led to her death.
   • The defense contend that the transfer of the major DNA profile was
     "passive" as it occurred 7 days previous to the crime event.

   In my opinion, the first explanation is more likely than the second
   explanation. This opinion is based upon three different observations,
   based on experimental results in the published scientific literature:

   • There is a very low probability (less than 5%) that a DNA profile will
     be observed 24 h after the contact that led to the transfer.
   • There is low probability (between 5% and 25%) that a DNA profile
     will be transferred by a cohabitee.
   • There is a low probability (less than 5%) that a DNA profile will be
     transferred by a random person

- There is a medium probability (between 25% and 75%) that a reportable DNA profile will be transferred by vigorous scratching provided that the fingernail scrapings are collected within 24 h.
  Note that the major profile is a foreign profile (not from Ms V) and the fact that this profile is major also supports the contention that transfer was "active," rather than "passive."

4. Taken in the context of the circumstances of this case and the relative strength of the major component to the DNA mixture, in my opinion the DNA profiling evidence in this case is readily explained and more likely if it had originated as a result of a recent primary transfer event, e.g., scratching between Ms V and Mr S close to the time of her death, rather than as a result of some other type of transfer event which happened 7 days previously or as a result of some unspecified secondary transfer from a biological material deposited in Ms V's house by Mr S on some previous occasion when they were in a relationship with each other.

5. It is important to reiterate that the statistic (one in one million) that has been provided is specific to the possible identity of the DNA profile itself; it cannot be used to infer the mode of transfer of the DNA profile.

Commentary: The final statement is apportioned into two parts: the first part addresses the strength of the DNA profiling evidence and the second part addresses the mode of transfer and the two sections are kept separate. This is because the strength of the DNA evidence cannot be used to infer the mode of transfer and vice versa. The model provided here shows how "expert-opinion" is underpinned by the experimental evidence which is constantly referred to throughout the report. By reporting probabilistic ranges, this also provides a court an indication of the "uncertainties" that are inherent with any opinion that is expressed. This process is demonstrably objective and the risks of "confirmation bias" are consequently reduced.

Recommendation 9: If a scientist expresses an opinion, then this opinion must be qualified by experimental evidence. If an opinion is expressed that appears to have no supporting evidence (in terms of peer-review or data-analysis) so that it cannot be tested objectively, then it has no scientific basis.

3.7 SUMMARY

The conclusions on transfer follow the likelihood ratio format as they address the prosecution and the defense propositions and the probabilities are derived from Table 3.1. There is a very low probability of observing a DNA profile originating from an "active" or "passive" method of transfer where there has been 7 days intervening vs. a medium probability of transfer via scratching so long as the sampling is immediate. We have to reiterate that the mode of transfer of the major (foreign) DNA profile is a separate consideration to the identity of the DNA profile itself. The prosecution contend that "active" transfer of the major DNA profile to underneath the fingernails of Ms V was coincident with the attack that led to her death, i.e., reference to Mr S as the possible assailant must be specifically avoided in this part of the statement. Conversely, the defense argument is two pronged: (a) The DNA profile addressed in part 1 is from an *unknown person* and this probability is calculated to be less than one in one million. (b) The second defense alternative accepts the possibility that the major profile is from Mr S, but the transfer was "passive" and innocent, occurring some 7 days before crime.

We also have the additional information that the major profile was a major component. From Matte et al. (2012), there was increased chance of observing a foreign DNA from "active" scratching and this is because more DNA is transferred by this method resulting in an increase in the profile attributable to the donor at time zero, by this method. Conversely, "passive" transfer would normally produce the minor component of the DNA profile. Note that over several hours the profile would decay to rapidly become the minor component, hence the window of opportunity to retrieve samples is limited. If the victim is dead, as in this case, then the event is effectively frozen at time zero.

A note of caution is required: the more sensitive the test, the longer DNA will persist and contamination events are more likely to occur. This is where the *relevance* of the experimental evidence is crucial to any conclusions that are put forward. It will be important to ensure that the methods reported in the literature are consistent with the specific method used in the case that is reported.

CHAPTER 4

National DNA Databases, Strength of Evidence and Error Rates

DNA databases are extremely powerful tools that can be used to detect perpetrators of crime. The power of the database search is derived from the ability to eliminate large numbers of innocent people from an investigation. There are pitfalls to consider: a wrongful inclusion (the false positive error) could lead to wrongful arrest and/or conviction; alternatively, the wrongful exclusion could lead to the false negative error where the perpetrator is undetected and potentially eliminated from the inquiry. Both can have serious consequences.

4.1 THE TESTING STRATEGY USED BY NATIONAL DNA DATABASES

Until very recently, most EU countries, including the United Kingdom, used a commercial system known as the second generation multiplex (SGM Plus^{TM}) to generate DNA profiles (Gill, 2002; Gill et al., 2006a,b). This system consists of 10 genetic markers or *loci* known as short tandem repeats (STRs). The genotype of an individual at each locus is comprised two *alleles* which may be the same or have separate identity. The STR genotype is converted into a series of 20 digits, where each digit signifies the identity or *type* of each *allele* that is based on the number of tandem repeating sequences. With this particular example, a complete DNA profile from a single contributor will provide a match probability of approximately 10^{-13} between two unrelated individuals. The methods used to designate DNA profiles are little changed from those originally devised for the UK national DNA database (NDNAD). However, many other multiplex systems are currently employed throughout Europe and there is consequently only partial overlap between the markers utilized. The *European Network of Forensic Science Institutes* (ENFSI) lists 43 kits that have been used, or are currently used in Europe (ENFSI, 2014). The recent implementation of new, more powerful, systems in 2013 across Europe along with EU agreements (Schneider, 2009), to expand the number of core loci has significantly reduced the chance of *adventitious matches* (i.e., matches with random individuals). However, DNA databases are retrospective, which means that most samples have been processed using the older (less efficient systems). It is impracticable to reprocess all old samples so that they are comparable with the most up-to-date tests. Consequently, the majority of database comparisons are still restricted to the first generation set of core loci. As older offenders are replaced by younger offenders, databases will naturally evolve, but we will need to wait 10 years before the full benefits of the new multiplexes can be fully realized.

4.2 THERE ARE TWO KINDS OF DNA DATABASES

There are two separate databases: the largest comprises reference samples (n_{ref}) from known individuals. The DNA sample is usually collected via a buccal scrape. This is a noninvasive method that uses a swab to remove surface cells from inside the mouth. This reference database is compared to a separately maintained database of crime stains (n_{cstain}). Comparisons are made to discover matches between the two databases (Figure 4.1) and if successful then the donor of the known reference sample becomes

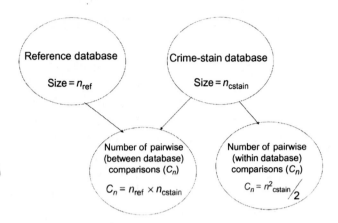

Figure 4.1 The national DNA database comprises two parts. The first is the reference database with n_{ref} samples and the second is the crime stain database of n_{cstain} samples. There are a total of $n_{ref} \times n_{cstain}$ comparisons, and approximately $n^2_{cstain}/2$ comparisons if the crime-stain database is searched for linked stains.

a suspect(s) or person of interest. Comparisons can also be carried out between samples within the crime-stain database in order to discover if crimes are linked to each other. This can establish the presence of serial offenders who may be undetected because they are absent from the reference sample database. A single individual may be responsible for many crimes and this is common with high-volume offences such as burglary. There is usually no requirement to carry out comparisons within the reference sample database of known individuals. Although the UK DNA database (June 2013) has about 6 million samples recorded in the reference database, only approximately 5 million of these are functional since 14% of the total are replicates (UK National DNA Database, 2013).

There are many texts that describe the biology of STR DNA profile in detail—the interested reader is referred to John Butler's books (e.g., Butler, 2005, 2009, 2011).

DNA profiles are stored in the form of a numeric code that is based on the nomenclature of each STR. The first NDNAD was started in 1995 by the United Kingdom and it is still by far the largest in Europe (ENFSI, 2014) but the databases of China and the United States are much larger. Referring to the United Kingdom as an example, there are currently 5 million reference samples (n_{ref}) that have been collected from suspects or known individuals and ca. 430,000 crime-stain profiles (n_{cstain}).

In the latest survey across Europe in 2013 (ENFSI, 2014), there were $n_{ref} = 9.83$ million profiles and $n_{cstain} = 1.39$ million crime-stain profiles.

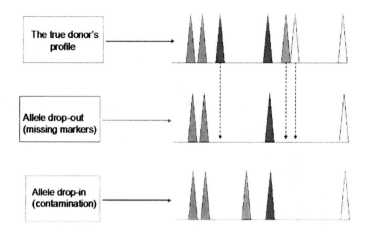

Figure 4.2 *This figure shows how the DNA profile may change because of the combinatorial effects of allele drop-out (where alleles are missing: dashed lines). Allele drop-in (contamination) results in additional alleles. The result is a DNA profile that is altered from the original and may result in false inclusions or false exclusions.*

The rate of growth of NDNADs is accelerating. Within 5–10 years, we can easily project that European databases will exceed 20 million reference samples, along with ca. 2 million crime stains. The next generation systems will potentially be used to evaluate databases of more than 100+ million people as reference samples.

Reference samples are generally non-problematic, because they are controls. Quality is not an issue. On the other hand, casework samples are compromised. The quality may be poor if the biological sample is limited in terms of quantity, or if it is degraded. Casework samples are not provided under clinical conditions. This means that interpretation of the crime stain requires special consideration (Figure 4.2):

- The sample may be partial—i.e., alleles or complete loci may be missing. This is known as allele or locus *drop-out* (Gill et al., 2000).
- The sample may be contaminated, i.e., additional alleles may be present. This is known as *drop-in* (Gill et al., 2000).
- The sample may be a mixture of two or more individuals; a complex profile is present that is challenging to resolve into its components.
- The alleles in the sample may be wrongly designated (Rand et al., 2004).

4.2.1 The Partial Profile

When the power of a DNA profiling system is discussed it is generally based upon the *full* DNA profile. This assumption is often not realistic (Gill and Buckleton, 2010; Gill et al., 2012; Hicks et al., 2010a); many case stains are partial. This means that alleles or markers are usually missing from the profile and the power to discriminate between individuals is substantially reduced.

Consequently, the chance that it will match a sample originating from a different individual is *increased*. The *adventitious match* leads to an error of *false inclusion* or *false positive* error. Adventitious matches can also occur with full profiles of course, but are less probable. Conversely, if a profile is wrongly designated by the scientist (or because of a contamination event known as *drop-in*), then it will not match a reference or crime-stain profile. This could also lead to an error of *false exclusion* or *false negative error*. In order to minimize the level of *false exclusions*, NDNADs also carry out *low stringency* searches—a complete match is not needed for a *putative* match to be inferred. A low stringency search typically involves discovering close matches: for example, a match between a reference profile and a crime stain profile at all but one allele. These are known as $n-1$ searches; out of a total of n-alleles, one allele is allowed as a "wildcard" mismatch. Sometimes searches are carried out at lower stringency by allowing more than one "wildcard" mismatch.

Paradoxically, *low stringency* tests intended to reduce *false exclusion* rates will *increase* the *false inclusion rate*. Some *false inclusions* will be detected at the second stage of testing (where biological samples are manually compared or reworked with different multiplexes).[1] Nevertheless, it follows that if the *false inclusion rate* is too high, it compromises the efficiency of a NDNAD, simply because the increased amount of work to investigate multiple matches is prohibitive.

4.3 HOW THE PITCHFORK CASE LED TO THE FIRST NATIONAL DNA DATABASE

The history of the DNA database began with the first crime solved by DNA profiling, namely: the notorious Narborough murders in 1987. This famous case is worth explaining in some detail, since the lessons learned are still pertinent. Two young girls, Lynda Mann and Dawn Ashworth, were murdered in the Narborough area of Leicestershire in 1983 and 1986, respectively. A suspect had been arrested and charged with murder.

---

[1] There may be commercial constraints to retesting samples, however, here it is strongly advocated as part of basic scientific principle that requires separate tests to reinforce conclusions.

Although he had admitted to the recent murder of Ashworth, he denied the earlier murder of Mann. As the two offences were believed to have been committed by the same perpetrator; the police were keen to use the recently invented method of DNA profiling. Alec Jeffreys processed the crime samples and found that they did not match the suspect who was therefore excluded. Since the police were convinced that they had found the perpetrator (after all, he had confessed to one murder), concerns were raised about the reliability of the tests and they asked for verification from the now defunct Forensic Science Service. The samples were duly reanalyzed, and the Jeffreys' conclusion was confirmed (Gill and Werrett, 1987). The suspect was released, as he had apparently confessed to a crime that he had not committed, but the problem remained to discover the identity of a serial killer who was likely to reoffend.

4.4 DEFINING THE "TARGET POPULATION"

Because the crime was a serious sexual assault by a male, all females, and those males who were too young or too old were automatically eliminated as suspects. This left a core group of approximately 5000 male suspects where each was considered equally likely to have committed the offence, i.e., there was no further background information to further separate them. This group of N males is called the "target population." Rounding the numbers for convenience, it is useful to begin by asking the question: If the perpetrator is one of 5000 individuals, and there is no information available to distinguish between them, what is the chance that any individual (i) is the perpetrator? This is called the *prior probability* of guilt, and it is easily calculated as 1 in 5000 (i.e., the size of the "target population" itself).

Since the police were convinced that the crime had been committed by a local resident, this meant that all $N = 5000$ males, who were between the ages of ca.18–60 within the target area, were considered as suspects. Once the target population was identified, the aim of the next stage of the investigation was to reduce the size of the suspect population of N individuals by serial elimination of suspects.[2] This was achieved by comparing their reference DNA profile with the crime-stain profiles to see if they matched. If n individuals can be eliminated from an inquiry, then the target population

---

[2] The process is similar to the method that modern databases use, except that comparisons are automated by computer algorithms, and the search is concurrent, rather than sequential. The principle of elimination of potential suspects by identifying exclusionary nonmatching DNA profiles is the same.

will correspondingly decrease to $N - n$, and the *prior probability* of 1 in $N - n$ of randomly selecting the perpetrator increases. We must be careful not to confuse the terms: perpetrator and suspect as they are quite different. If a crime has been committed, then a perpetrator exists whose identity is either unknown or unconfirmed. The purpose of the scientific and police investigation is to identify the pool of suspects that is believed to include the perpetrator and to eliminate all but one person. The court then decides the ultimate issue of guilt vs. innocence. Only if a guilty verdict is returned, will the perpetrator be considered as "known" (if a verdict is quashed or overturned, then the perpetrator is "unknown" once more, and the court has erroneously returned a false positive identification).

In the Narborough murders inquiry, the decision was made to collect blood samples from all of the males within the target population. Note that since DNA profiling was in its infancy at the time and the DNA database did not exist. It was necessary to restrict the target group because resources to carry out the analysis were limited. None of the "high throughput" benefits of automation that exist today had been invented. However, traditional blood typing (ABO and PGM enzyme) was feasible. Using these methods, it was possible to eliminate 4000 individuals from the target population, leaving a total of 1000 individuals to analyze using DNA profiling, increasing the *prior probability* to 1 in 1000. All of this work was carried out at the Home Office Lab at Aldermaston, UK.

Updating the Information

This is the first example of *updating* the information. This process is crucial to any investigation and it is built into the statistical framework described here. The first question is: What is the chance of selecting the perpetrator at random from some target population? The starting position, in the absence of any other information, was probability of guilt of 1 in 5000 against any particular individual. By process of elimination, the blood grouping information reduces the target population to 1000 individuals. Consequently, the probability increases to 1 in 1000.

However, no match was discovered—effectively all 5000 individuals were eliminated. It initially implied that the perpetrator must be outside the target population of males. A temporary dead-end had been reached.

The surprising breakthrough came later on, when one of Pitchfork's colleagues, Ian Kelly, from the bakery where he worked, was overheard talking about the case in a pub. He had been persuaded by Pitchfork to provide a sample, using his passport substituted with Kelly's photograph as false identity. This conversation was reported to the police and Pitchfork was forced to provide a blood sample that proved him to be the perpetrator—this meant that he had been correctly identified as part of the "target population" of 5000 males, but the methods used to verify identity were clearly insufficient. Nevertheless, without the DNA screen, the perpetrator would not have been discovered. The case was remarkable in that it literally laid the groundwork for the future of DNA profiling strategy, and simultaneously illustrated the benefits and some of the pitfalls:

- It demonstrated that a DNA database was a useful way to eliminate large numbers of people as suspects. In the case described, Pitchfork was the only suspect within the target population who had a DNA profile that matched. All other members of the group did not match.
- However, an error of person identification had wrongly eliminated the perpetrator.

In the following discussion it is assumed that profiles have been correctly identified, i.e., there are no interpretation errors. Later in Section 4.24, the effect of errors is explored and the potential implications are discussed. Some simple statistics are introduced since it is important to ensure that the discussion is firmly rooted in a coherent framework.

4.5 DATABASES ARE NOT ALWAYS NEEDED TO SOLVE CRIMES

Two kinds of crime types can be categorized:

- *Type I*: The suspect is apprehended because of non-DNA evidence and the DNA is corroborative.
- *Type II*: The suspect is identified as the result of a DNA search and the non-DNA evidence is corroborative.

Examples are as follows (*Type I* is deliberately made extreme to make the point clear):

Type I: A burglar has been apprehended running from crime scene clutching a bag full of silverware taken from a house—let us assume that he also cut himself on a broken window and left a blood deposit that becomes the crime-stain evidence. We assume an unequivocal complete match. There is also fingerprint evidence and some distinctive fibers. He was arrested in possession of the goods but denied the offence claiming to have found the silverware in the road. The background information (non-DNA evidence) is nevertheless highly probative and this forms the basis of the primary evidence against him. The DNA profiling evidence is corroborative and is therefore secondary evidence. The *type I* crime is typified by one or more crime stains and the presence of non-DNA evidence. The DNA comparisons do not require the DNA database to discover a perpetrator.

* *Type-I characteristics*: The non-DNA evidence is primary and strongly implicates the suspect; the prior probability of guilt is already high and the DNA evidence is corroborative. A database search is not required to link the DNA profile with the suspect.

Type-II crimes are committed by an unknown perpetrator, as demonstrated by the Pitchfork example. A pool of suspects from a target population is investigated. The DNA database may be considered to represent a subset of this pool since not everyone in the target population is held on the database. Consequently, the DNA profiling evidence becomes the primary evidence in the case, and the non-DNA evidence becomes corroborative—which is the reverse of the *type-I* crime. However, if a match occurs as a result of a search of the NDNAD, then the meaning of a match still requires to be considered within the context of the case. The fact of the database search does not cancel the requirement to consider the non-DNA evidence in the same detail.

* *Type-II characteristics*: A database search is necessary to discover the suspect. The non-DNA evidence may be considered corroborative to the DNA profiling evidence. The DNA search is an exploratory method which identifies potential suspects. Once identified the investigation may find additional non-DNA evidence to corroborate. Alternatively, the DNA evidence may be "sole-plank" or very limited, in which case the DNA evidence may stand-alone (however, it is not advisable to put forward DNA evidence without corroboration).

4.6 MISCONCEPTIONS

* It may be commonly believed that a DNA profile provides "unique identification," but this is untrue. The DNA profile is often described as partial which means that alleles are missing as a result of degradation, or DNA is present at low level. Extra alleles may also occur because of the "drop-in" phenomenon and because DNA profiles are often present in admixture.
* The presence of a DNA profile is not necessarily associated with the crime event or the guilt of a suspect. In Section 5.12, there is a discussion about the various modes of transfer of DNA profiling evidence.

• It is noted that the power of databases relies as much upon the power to eliminate individuals as suspects, as well as to include them. However, there is error in all databases. There is no such thing as certainty of exclusion, or certainty of inclusion, yet many commentators have assumed this to be true.

4.7 THE STRENGTH OF EVIDENCE EXPRESSED AS A MATCH PROBABILITY

It is tempting to think in terms of a DNA "match," or "inclusion," that supports the prosecution hypothesis of guilt, or a non-match, exclusion, that supports the defense hypothesis of innocence. However, it is an oversimplification to think in terms of black and white as the reality—it is somewhere in between: "shades of grey," where there is an entire spectrum of possibilities between the two extremes.

Strength of Evidence, Wording

Note the wording used here to express the strength of evidence is specific: *the strength of the evidence that supports the prosecution hypothesis of inclusion* or the *defense hypothesis of exclusion*:

• For court reporting, a subtle but important point is that the discussion is focussed on whether the evidence *supports* the prosecution or defense hypotheses in order to avoid the prosecutor's fallacy—an error of logic (Balding and Donnelly, 1994).
• Traditionally, large numbers, e.g., 1 in 1 billion are quoted in favor of the prosecution hypothesis, but if we think in terms of a "sliding scale" then, it is also appropriate to estimate a numeric strength of evidence to support the alternative defense hypothesis of exclusion. Traditionally, statistics are only provided in favor of a prosecution hypothesis—if the evidence is weak or inconclusive then a crime stain will be verbally dismissed as inconclusive or an exclusion. However, with new interpretation methods such as "LRmix" (Haned, 2011; Haned and Gill, 2011) (Section 5.7.1), these terms are either unnecessary or can be qualified by a number.[a] It is no longer necessary to think in black and white terms of "match" vs. "nonmatch" or inclusion vs. exclusion (Gill and Buckleton, 2010).

---

[a]For example, we could state: "the evidence is 1 billion times more likely to support the defense hypothesis of exclusion."

Authorities may be unwilling to mount a prosecution that depends upon DNA profiling evidence of anything that is considered to be "low strength of evidence," e.g., **less** than **one** in one million *or* one in **less** than **one** million (to avoid a common confusion, the words "less" and "one" are shown in bold type to emphasize the dependency of the two words).[3] However, all decisions that are made on the basis of some threshold are arbitrary. Provided that the calculations are correct there is no reason to discount a low number as "insufficient evidence" so long as the model used to interpret is reasonable.

4.8 CONCLUSION

In principle, there should be no difference between the probative values of strength of evidence derived via *type I* or *type II* crimes—this is in keeping with a statistical principle—namely, the order in which the evidence is assessed does not matter (Balding, 2005, p. 28). However, the distinction is made here to remind us that the presence of a DNA profile match does not mean that the other (non-DNA) evidence in the case is any less important. The *type I* crime starts with non-DNA evidence and the DNA is corroborative. With the *type II* crime, the danger arises if the identification is made from a search of the NDNAD and the non-DNA evidence is ignored leading to the "confirmation bias" associated with the "the naïve investigator effect," where the DNA evidence may be overweighted in relation to any exculpatory evidence that may exist.

4.8.1 The Naïve Investigator Effect
The definition is expanded in Section 1.5.3: the naïve investigator finds the closest match to a crime stain in a NDNAD, he ignores exculpatory evidence and seeks to prosecute the matching individual, ignoring other evidence in the case.

Recommendation 10: To mitigate the effect of the confirmation bias, the assessment of the non-DNA evidence should be carried out independently of the DNA evidence.

---

[3]Otherwise an error is easily made—illustrated in a recent UK government document on DNA profiling http://www.official-documents.gov.uk/document/cm87/8750/8750.pdf where it erroneously states on page 11: "It uses a DNA profiling system that gives random match probabilities of in excess of one in a billion"; it should read, either: "less than one in a billion" or "one in greater than a billion."

4.9 SEARCHING ENTIRE DATABASES (EFFECTIVENESS LINKED TO THE ADVENTITIOUS MATCH)

With partial DNA profiles, it is likely that one or more adventitious (chance) matches will arise when searched against a large DNA database. If the true donor is concurrently absent from the database, it will increase the risks of miscarriage of justice for *type II* cases, especially if the non-DNA evidence in a case is weak or non-existent.

Consider a search of an entire UK database of 5 million people vs. 430,000 crime stains, it is interesting to measure the expected performance of a database as follows:

- How many reference profiles will adventitiously match a crime stain per search?
- How many historical adventitious matches would be expected for all database comparisons ever made (430,000 stains compared against 5 million reference samples)?

Table 4.1 shows why it is necessary to "upgrade" multiplexes to more powerful discriminatory versions. The original SGM multiplex utilized up to year 2000 only had a full profile discriminating power of 1 in 50 million. If this was still in use, then every comparison made would provide (on average) 1 false positive matches every 10 searches. The new multiplexes introduced throughout Europe have much lower match probabilities (average 10^{-19}). As databases grow in size, the much improved discriminating power will mitigate the effects of the exponential growth of

Table 4.1 For a 5 Million Sample Reference Database There Is a Low Risk of a False Positive Match for a Full DNA Profile.

	No. of comparisons	Match probability					
		1.00E−13	1.00E−10	1.00E−06	1.00E−05	1.00E−04	1.00E−03
Expected number of false positive matches per crime stain	5,000,000	0.00	0.00	5	50	500	5000
Historical false positive matches	2.15E + 12	2.15E − 01	2.15E + 02	2.15E + 06	2.15E + 07	2.15E + 08	2.15E + 09

If the profile is partial with a match probability of 1 in 1 million then approximately 5 false positives are expected per database search. The historical false positive rate is the number of false positives when the entire crime-stain database is of 430,000 samples compared with the reference database of 5 million samples, a total of 2.15×10^{12} comparisons. This is just within the limits of the full profile SGM Plus system. There are 0.2 historical full profile matches expected. 'E' is a shortcut excel notation that means × 10 raised to a power indicated to the right of the expression.

very large databases, but there will still be a significant false positive rate when partial profiles are searched.

It is important to note that the calculations above only refer to unrelated people. As databases grow, it becomes much more likely that matches will occur between related individuals (e.g., cousins; Weir, 2006).

4.10 HOW DOES A SEARCH OF A NDNAD AFFECT THE STRENGTH OF EVIDENCE?

4.10.1 The Perpetrator Lives in a Known Population of Known Size

Databases are extraordinarily powerful instruments. But all methods have limitations that need to be identified, highlighted, measured, and their significance explained. A "psychology" has emerged that can attach almost mystical value to the fact of the "matching" DNA profile—media and "CSI" TV shows reinforce the misleading (cognitive biased) viewpoint that the mere presence of a DNA profile provides direct proof that the suspect committed the crime.

The discussion now turns to the mitigation or prevention of "confirmation bias." The case of wrongful arrest of Adam Scott shows the role of the investigator to be the weakest link in the chain.

4.10.2 The Role of the Investigator

A distinction must be made between the processes of *investigation* vs. the *court* process to determine the ultimate issue of guilt or innocence. The investigator comprises a team of police and scientific experts, who collaborate with each other in order to *evaluate* the evidence. Once the investigative phase is completed, the prosecuting authorities decide whether there is sufficient evidence that can be put to a court in order for there to be a reasonable chance of conviction. To do this an informal nonstatistical assessment is made of *probability of guilt*.[4] If a prosecution is taken forward, lawyers decide *how* to present the evidence to the court; scientific witnesses are called in order to explain the significance of findings and to interpret

---

[4]Note that prosecutors decide whether an individual has a reasonable chance of prosecution, hence it is appropriate to directly evaluate $Pr(G)$.

the evidence. The purpose of the court is to evaluate the strength of the evidence that has been put forward by the various "actors." Scientific experts strongly affect the outcome of a trial so it is important to ensure that the methods used to give opinions are objective and standardized as much as possible.

Since the fact of a "matching DNA profile" can be overweighted in relation to exculpatory evidence, it is necessary to focus the investigation from a different point of view. Statistically, it does not matter in which order the DNA vs. non-DNA evidence is evaluated, but here it is argued, in the interests of minimizing risks of cognitive bias by experts and courts, that the strength of non-DNA evidence against a suspect(s) should be ideally be considered *before* the DNA profiling evidence.

Currently, the investigative system is geared to work the opposite way round—starting with the DNA evidence first, applying the non-DNA evidence second. The way forward is to split the investigation so that the strength of the non-DNA evidence is assessed separately, in absence of the knowledge of the DNA profile. Once this has been done, the combined strength of evidence will be less prone to the effect of "confirmation bias."

The perpetrator must live in some population which can easily be defined in geographic terms (e.g., an entire country or regions within a country). As an extreme, the entire population of the world could be considered. Whereas we are certain that the perpetrator is part of this population with probability = 100%, it is excessive; it is extremely unlikely that a crime committed in the United Kingdom has been committed by a person resident in Northern Tibet. The world population is not usually relevant. From the perspective of the investigator, the target population must be localized and minimized in order to make the investigation manageable.

There will often be a subset of the population that is relevant—returning to the Narborough murders as an example, we can ask:

What is the prior probability of guilt of any individual (i) *in a population of size* N, *in the absence of the DNA evidence and any other information?*

- The crime was committed in the United Kingdom where there were $N = 60$ million people resident. One was the perpetrator. The *prior probability* of guilt was 1 in 60 million.

- The crime was sexual assault so females are excluded and the perpetrator is in the male population. This reduces the relevant population to $N = 30$ million. The *prior probability* was increased to 1 in 30 million.
- The crime was committed in the Narborough area—there was strong evidence to suggest that the perpetrator was local and this further restricts the population of males to approximately $N = 5000$ individuals (restricted to the ca. 18–60 age group). The *prior probability* was increased further to 1 in 5000.
- Therefore, the size of the target population of suspects has been greatly reduced in size, by updating the information. Before the DNA evidence, the *prior probability of guilt* was increased from 1 in 60 *million* to 1 in 5000.

As the investigation proceeded, the information was continually *updated*. Later it is shown how this information can be combined with the DNA evidence to provide a much more mature overview of the evidence.

4.11 FOCUSSING THE INVESTIGATION (ELIMINATING MORE SUSPECTS FROM THE TARGET POPULATION): INTRODUCING THE CONCEPT OF "WEIGHTS"

To recap, each member of the target population is considered to be equally likely to be the perpetrator, before the additional knowledge provided by the DNA search. The purpose of this section is to introduce the concept of *a priori* "weighting" to show how the target group can be further subdivided into subgroups, where individuals within each group are more or less likely to have committed the offence relative to a defined suspect.

To be consistent, the explanation and notation provided by Balding (2005, p. 24) is followed. Consider an individual i within the target population that is chosen as a suspect $i = s$, and relative to that suspect, all other individuals $i = 2 \ldots N$ are assigned a "weighting." The weighting gives the probability that a different i^{th} individual is more or less likely to be the perpetrator than the suspect, before the DNA evidence is evaluated. In an investigation with few or no leads, it will be usual to apply an equivalent weighting $w_{i,s} = 1$ so that any of the other individuals, $i = 2 \ldots N$, chosen for comparison from within the target group is considered to be equally likely to have committed the offence. The term $w_{i,s}$ expresses the *weighting* in support of, or against, the guilt of individual i relative to the suspect s, given the *background information* E_o and excluding the *genetic information* E_{dna}

$$w_{i,s}(E_o) = \frac{P(C = i|E_o)}{P(C = s|E_o)} \tag{4.1}$$

where C is the perpetrator, i is a possible defendant other than the suspect, and E_o is the background information; $w_{i,s}$ is the weight of the non-DNA evidence against a person i in the target population, relative to its weight against the suspect.

If $w_{i,s} > 1$ then this means, *a priori*, that the individual i is more likely to be the perpetrator than the suspect, whereas if $w_{i,s} < 1$ then the converse is true.

Using a simple Bayes theorem derivation: Balding (2005, p. 25) described as the "strength of evidence formula" in the absence of a DNA profile is:

$$Pr(G|E_{dna}, E_o) = \frac{1}{1 + \sum_1^{N-1} w_{i,s}R_{i,s}} \tag{4.2}$$

where $R_{i,s}$ is the likelihood ratio (LR) (note that the numerator evaluates the defense hypothesis and the denominator evaluates the prosecution hypothesis in this notation):

$$
\begin{aligned}
R_{i,s} &= \frac{\Pr(E_{dna}C = i, E_o)}{\Pr(E_{dna}C = s, E_o)} \\
&= \frac{p}{1} = p
\end{aligned}
$$

where the summation ($\sum$) is across all possible alternatives to the suspect in population $N - 1$. The suspect(s) is chosen and assigned $Pr = 1$ under the prosecution hypothesis (Hp). Parameter $w_{i,s}$ is defined by Eqn 4.1 and p is the match probability of the DNA profile.

From Eqn 4.2, if $w_{i,s} = 1$ for all members of target population $N - 1$, then Eqn 4.1 simplifies:

$$
\begin{aligned}
Pr(G|E_{dna}, E_o) &= \frac{1}{1 + \sum_1^{N-1} w_{i,s}R_{i,s}} \\
&= \frac{1}{1 + p \times (N - 1)} \\
P(G|E_{dna}, E_o) &\approx \frac{1}{1 + Np} \tag{4.3}
\end{aligned}
$$

Now it will be shown how weighting the evidence can be used to place the DNA profiling evidence into perspective of the population size.

4.12 THE CASE OF R. v. ADAMS

The case of R. v. Adams is informative, since this was the focus of several appeal-court hearings and retrials. Adams was convicted of the offence of rape at trial and at each of the retrials. A comprehensive discussion of the case can be found by Lynch and McNally (2003).

The main evidence was from a DNA profile, a match probability of 1 in 200 million was reported, and the match was discovered by a database trawl in 1995. This was an embryonic database that was maintained by the Metropolitan Police Laboratory which was a local precursor to the NDNAD. It comprised just a few thousand samples. The case was the first *type II* example cited in Section 4.5. In common with many other cases discussed in this book, without the DNA evidence it was acknowledged that there would be insufficient evidence to convict.

The case was highly contentious because there was compelling exculpatory non-DNA evidence which countered the DNA evidence:

- The victim failed to identify the suspect in a "line-up."
- The victim stated that the defendant did not look like the man who attacked her and he did not fit the description that she gave of her attacker. She stated that he appeared to be older than her attacker.
- Adams stated that he had spent the entire evening with his girlfriend during the time of the attack and the alibi witness was not discredited.

The prosecution and defense scientists collaborated with each other to provide a questionnaire for the jury to fill in the answers to the probabilities to questions. Here I just consider the first question since it is the first example where the evidence of the target population was combined with the DNA evidence. The question put to the court was:

What is the chance, assuming nothing else about the case, that the rapist came from the local area?

A Verbatim Copy of the Evidence Provided to the Court

What is the chance, assuming nothing else about the case, that the rapist came from the local area? Donnelly cited local council data that 153,000 men between ages of 18 and 60 lived within a 15-km radius of the crime scene. For purposes of calculation, he rounded off this figure to 150,000. He then gave an illustrative estimate of a 75 percent chance that the attacker was a local man. Donnelly then divided 150,000 by 0.75, resulting in a figure of 200,000. According to the undisputed facts of the case, Adams was a local man so that *in the absence of any other evidence* the odds of his being the man who "shed" the semen sample recovered during the victim's examination were 200,000 to 1. Donnelly explained this procedure as follows:

> The ... rationale is that if we were certain it was a local man and there are 153,000 relevant local men, the fact that it is a particular one, Mr. Adams, we would assess as 1 over 150,000. If we are not certain it is a local man, our assessment for a particular local man will be decreased a bit. The way that changes is that you take your 150,000 which are the odds, 150,000 to 1—are the odds on innocence—and you increase that by 100 divided by the percentage, 75 percent ... We have now changed to a situation where our odds on a particular local man, Mr. Adams, is the one of interest, but a particular local man being the true rapist is 200,000 to one now.

4.13 CALCULATION USING THE WEIGHT OF EVIDENCE FORMULATION

Before considering the DNA evidence, Professor Donnelly estimated a 75% probability that the perpetrator was local and originated from a target population of "local" suspects of 150,000, each was considered to be equally likely to have committed the offence. The chance that the perpetrator was from outside the target population was therefore 25%. He did not consider the size of the "outside population" and it is not necessary to estimate, but here we expand the argument to include this consideration in order to build the discussion toward an evaluation of multiple populations where the weightings differ between them.

4.13.1 Weights Within the Target Population

The weights are calculated per individual, so if there are $n - 1 = 149,999$ individuals in a population, other than the suspect, and each is equally likely to be the perpetrator then the probability of any given individual being the perpetrator is $1/150,000$. Individuals cannot be distinguished hence the relative weighting $w_{i,s} = 1$.

Recall Eqn 4.1:

$$w_{i,s}(E_o) = \frac{P(C = i|E_o)}{P(C = s|E_o)} = 1$$

4.13.2 Weights Outside the Target Population

There are $N-n = 30$ million$-150,000$ men in the United Kingdom "outside population" and *within* each individual (a) within this cohort is considered to be equally likely to be the perpetrator—each is assigned *a prior* probability of guilt $P(C = a|E_o) = 1/N - n = 1/29,850,000$. If a suspect was drawn from outside the target population, relative to all other individuals from the same group, the weighting applied would be $w_{a,s} = 1$ since there is nothing to distinguish between each of them.

4.13.3 Calculating Weights Between Two Different Populations

Following the Adams example, we are provided with the additional information that there is a 75% chance that the perpetrator is from the target population and 25% chance that he is from outside the target group.

Since we consider the relative "guilt" of each ith individual in turn, these probabilities are shared between each individual within each of the populations:

1. $P(C = i|E_o)$ or $P(C = s|E_o)$, for each male within the target population is:
   $0.75/150,000 = 5 \times 10^{-6}$
2. $P(C = a|E_o)$, for each male outside the target population is:
   $0.25/(30,000,000 - 150,000) = 8.38 \times 10^{-9}$.

Given that s is from the "target population," the weighting relative to individual a taken from outside the target population is calculated as:

$$w_{a,s}(E_o) = \frac{P(C = a|E_o)}{P(C = s|E_o)}$$

$$w_{a,s}(E_o) = \frac{8.38 \times 10^{-9}}{5 \times 10^{-6}}$$

$$w_{a,s}(E_o) = \frac{1}{597} \tag{4.4}$$

- Before the DNA evidence is assessed, a person from outside the target group a is 597 times less likely than a suspect taken from the target group to be the perpetrator.

The weight of evidence formula described by Balding is expanded to incorporate the weights for the "within" and "outside" target populations:

$$P(G|E_o) = \frac{1}{1 + (n-1)w_{i,s = \text{within}} + (N-n)w_{a,s = \text{outside}}} \quad (4.5)$$

Considering the *entire* population of 30 *million* males of the United Kingdom, the overall probability of guilt can be updated to evaluate the strength of evidence against a suspect who has been drawn from within the target population. Plugging the figures into Eqn 4.5:

$$P(G|E_o) \quad = \quad \frac{1}{1 + (150,000 - 1) \times 1 + (30,000,000 - 150,000) \times 1/597}$$

$$P(G|E_o) \quad = \quad 1/200,000 \quad\quad (4.6)$$

- We have recovered the answer expressed as odds by Professor Donnelly where he stated: *We have now changed to a situation where our odds on a particular local man, Mr. Adams, is the one of interest, but a particular local man being the true rapist is 200,000 to one now [against].*

4.14 HOW DOES THE WEIGHTING ALTER $P(G|E_0)$ IF THE SUSPECT IS TAKEN FROM OUTSIDE THE TARGET POPULATION?

Now suppose that the suspect has been apprehended from outside the target population. The following probabilities do not change:

1. $P(C = i|E_o)$, for each male within the target population is the same: $0.75/150,000 = 5 \times 10^{-6}$
2. $P(C = a|E_o)$ or $P(C = s|E_o)$, for each male outside the target population is the same: $0.25/(30,000,000 - 150,000) = 8.38 \times 10^{-9}$.
3. Because s is now located in the "outside population," this weighting changes. Now: $w_{a,s} = 1$, as these individuals cannot be distinguished. Since it was considered to be considerably more likely that the perpetrator was localized within the "target population," this means that *any individual i* from this group is $w_{i,s} = 597$ times *more likely* than a suspect from the outside group (a), to be the perpetrator.

Therefore, we evaluate:

$$P(G|E_o) = \frac{1}{1 + (N)w_{i,s\,=\,\text{within}} + (N - n - 1)w_{a,s\,=\,\text{outside}}}$$

$$P(G|E_o) = \frac{1}{1 + (150,000) \times 597 + (30,000,000 - 150,000 - 1) \times 1}$$

$$P(G|E_o) = 1 \text{ in } 119 \text{ million} \tag{4.7}$$

(i.e., very strongly favors the defense, *before* considering the DNA evidence).

This simple demonstration shows that the probabilities alter dramatically if the suspect originated from outside the target population (the example is deliberately extreme to make the point—it would usually be possible to reasonably eliminate a substantial proportion of the male population of the United Kingdom based on age, geographic location, etc.).

4.15 RELEVANCE TO MISCARRIAGES OF JUSTICE RELATING TO THE NAÏVE INVESTIGATOR EFFECT

Recall the wrongful arrest of Adam Scott. A *type II* case. *A priori*, he was clearly outside the target population, had never visited the city where the crime had occurred, and lived hundreds of miles away. This case is classic example of "the naïve investigator effect" introduced in Section 1.5.3. He was a member of a cohort of individuals where the weighting applied would be very much lower than for an individual from the local population, but investigators did not take this into account.

So far the DNA evidence has been deliberately put to one side in order to reinforce the requirement to consider the non-DNA evidence first. Now we turn to the effect of updating the information using the DNA profiling evidence itself.

4.16 THE EFFECT OF UPDATING THE EVIDENCE USING DNA PROFILING (SUSPECT CHOSEN FROM WITHIN THE TARGET POPULATION)

The information of the DNA profiling evidence was omitted in order to preclude the effect of "confirmation bias" to reduce the risks that the strength of evidence of the DNA profile may be overweighted in relation to the "other" non-DNA evidence in the case.

In R. v. Adams, a crime stain E_{dna} had been typed and it matched the genotype of the suspect. Using Balding's notation, $R_{i,s}$ can be interpreted as a match probability:

$$R_{i,s}(E_{dna}|C, E_o) \;=\; \frac{P(E_{dna}|C = i, E_o)}{P(E_{dna}|C = s, E_o)}$$

$$R_{i,s} \;=\; \frac{1}{200\,\text{million}} \tag{4.8}$$

The evidence against s is easily assessed relative to the "target population" of 150,000, by multiplying with $R_{i,s}$ as follows:

$$P(G|E_{dna}, E_o) \;=\; \frac{1}{1 + (n-1)w_{i,s}R_{i,s}}$$

$$P(G|E_{dna}, E_o) \;=\; \frac{1}{1 + (150,000 - 1) \times 1/200\,\text{million}}$$

$$P(G|E_{dna}, E_o) \;=\; 99.926\%$$

$$\text{Odds}(G) \;=\; 1333 : 1 \tag{4.9}$$

Note that odds are calculated from probabilities: $\text{Odds} = p/1 - p$ and are included here for comparison.

Expanded to incorporate the evidence of the outside population:

$$P(G|E_{dna}, E_o) \;=\; \frac{1}{1 + (n-1)w_{i,s\,=\,\text{within}}R_{i,s} + (N-n)w_{a,s\,=\,\text{outside}}R_{i,s}}$$

$$P(G|E_{dna}, E_o) \;=\; \frac{1}{\begin{array}{c} 1 + (150,000 - 1) \times 1/200\,\text{million} + \\ (30\,\text{million} - 150,000) \times 1/(597 \times 200\,\text{million}) \end{array}}$$

$$P(G|E_{dna}, E_o) \;=\; 99.90\%$$

$$\text{Odds}(G) \;=\; 1000 : 1 \tag{4.10}$$

In fact, incorporating the evidence of the 30 *million* unknown males from the outside population has little effect on the combined strength of the evidence, reducing from 99.926% to 99.90%.

- It is important therefore to define the size of the "target population," the outside population has little effect provided that the probability of the perpetrator coming from the latter group is small.
- Given that the prosecution authorities will only prosecute an individual provided that there is a realistic chance of conviction, the ultimate issue of $P(G|E_{dna}, E_o)$, is an assessment that is directly relevant to investigators.

4.16.1 The Effect on the Strength of Evidence If Adams Had Originated from Outside the Target Population

If the same calculation was carried out if Adams had hypothetically been selected from the outside population, then the strength of evidence is much reduced. The probability of guilt, before the DNA evidence, is now $P(G|E_o) = 1$ in 119 million (Eqn 4.7) and this is an overwhelming consideration when the combined strength of evidence is calculated:

$$P(G|E_{dna}, E_o) = \frac{1}{1 + (150,000) \times 597 \times 1/200\,\text{million}} $$
$$+ (30,000,000 - 150,000 - 1) \times 1/200\,\text{million}$$

$$P(G|E_{dna}, E_o) = 62.6\%$$

$$\text{Odds}(G) = 1.7 : 1 \quad \text{(evidence very weakly favors prosecution)}$$

$$(4.11)$$

- Remember that the weights are always conditioned on an individual from the relevant population group relative to the suspect.
- In the wrongful arrest of Adam Scott, he originated from outside the target population and his prior probability of guilt was consequently low on this basis alone.
- The calculations are not intuitive and it is difficult to surmise that a jury or untrained investigator can adequately compensate the DNA statistic without using the quantitative methods described here.
- Intuition is prone to cognitive biases and in practice a court will have no guidance to place a numeric strength of evidence estimate from a DNA profile into context of exculpatory non-numeric, non-DNA evidence. It is inevitable that the DNA evidence will be overweighted. I have introduced a new term to describe this as the "swamping effect." It is part of the recognized family of cognitive biases: "Neglect of the prior base rates effect" which is defined as the *tendency to fail to incorporate prior known probabilities that are pertinent to the decision at hand* (Koehler, 1996).

4.17 THE SWAMPING EFFECT

4.17.1 Definition

Swamping Effect—Definition

The LR of the DNA profiling evidence is often quoted in the "billions." This very high figure tends to reinforce "confirmation bias," by disproportionately countering the exculpatory (non-numeric) non-DNA evidence that may favor the innocence of a suspect. In order to counterbalance cognitive biases, a scientific approach to quantitatively evaluate non-DNA evidence is required. A Bayesian framework is needed to facilitate a numeric evaluation of the combined evidence. The strength of evidence from different evidence types cannot be reliably combined by intuitive means because the results are often counter-intuitive.

4.18 IS THERE A SCIENTIFIC BASIS TO DEFINE "WEIGHTS" USING "GEOGRAPHIC PROFILING"?

Professor Donnelly's original proposal to subdivide the population into a "target group" and an "outside group" does have a solid scientific basis that to date has not been exploited in relation to DNA profiling evidence. Courts are amenable to the idea of a target population but have yet to incorporate it into the calculation (e.g., R. v. Wilkinson and the appeal-court statement described in Section 4.21.1).

A large amount of research has been carried out into "geographic profiling." This is a method that evaluates the *modus operandi* of the crime. The perpetrator of the Narborough murders had the hallmark of a serial killer—the murders were less than half a mile from each other, both were sexually motivated murders of young girls. Furthermore, the crimes were committed on footpaths that were used primarily by locals as shortcut routes (Figure 4.3). Therefore, these areas were less likely to be used and for that reason the perpetrator was less likely to be detected and was an ideal "hunting ground."

Previous studies have shown that serial killers tend to live very close to the crime scenes. Spatial analysis has been previously shown to be a valuable tool to use during the criminal investigation process—a number of software solutions have evolved for investigators to use. Although different types of crime may involve different behavior patterns of the offender, part of the expert investigator skills will be to categorize the type of crime to localize the residence of the perpetrator to areas that can be defined by

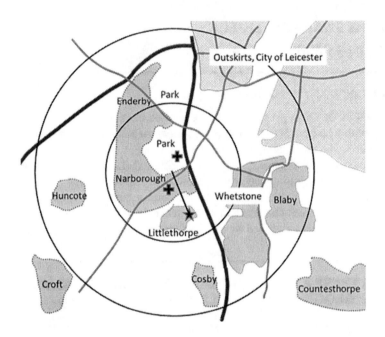

Figure 4.3 A schematic map showing villages and major roads. Concentric circles, increasing 1 mile radius, show the target population which defined the Pitchfork dragnet. Locations of the crimes are shown as crosses relative to the nearby location of the residence of the perpetrator in the village of Littlethorpe (shown by the star).

concentric probability zones. For example, Kent et al. (2006) focus on the serial killer:

- The perpetrator must feel comfortable with being able to commit the offence, and therefore needs to be familiar with the area of the crime so that the risks of detection are minimized.
- 301 serial killer homicide cases were analyzed by Kent et al. (2006). By plotting the distributions of the killer's residence relative to the center of the crime activities, it was demonstrated that more than half of all homicides were committed within 1 mile of the perpetrator's residence. The maximum distance that a perpetrator is willing to travel is approximately 12 miles using the shortest route, and just over 25 min in travel time using the quickest route.
- The likelihood of the perpetrator residence relative to the crime location can be modeled by an exponential decay function for distances >0.5 miles from the crime scenes.

Applying the probabilistic approach of Kent to the Narborough murder investigation, the weightings $w_{i,s}$ can easily be calculated (Figure 4.4). There is $Pr = 0.54$ that the perpetrator lived within 1 mile of offences

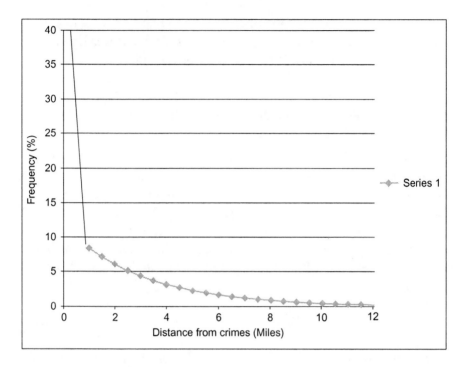

Figure 4.4 The Kent et al. (2006) frequency distribution showing the probability that a perpetrator lives within x miles from the crime location. Based on studies of 301 crimes.

and $Pr = 0.77$ that he lived within the 2 mile zone (this was where the dragnet was carried out). The 2–12 mile radius incorporates the city of Leicester and an approximate relevant population (16–64 years of age) is given as 100,000 from the city census. These individuals would share a *prior* probability = 0.22 between each of them, i.e. the prior probability of guilt per individual is very low: 0.22/100,000. The chance that the perpetrator lived outside the 12 mile radius is 0.007 shared between a population of 20 million in and outside the 12 mile radius is lower still: prior probability per individual = 0.001/20 million.

In previous examples there were two subdivisions of the general population into "target" and "outside." There is no restriction on the number of subgroups that can be applied. Each geographic location can be associated with a population size and a weighting specified by the probability that the perpetrator's residence is located in a particular region. If the crime type was such that it indicated that the offender was highly mobile then this may predicate a single target population to encompass the entire United Kingdom or beyond.

However, the framework described here is completely flexible to accommodate any scenario envisaged. It is really an issue for the investigator using sound data analysis to provide the necessary probabilities.

4.19 THE EFFECT OF A DATABASE SEARCH ON THE STRENGTH OF THE EVIDENCE

There has been much debate about the meaning of a (*type II*) match that is derived from a search of a NDNAD (see Buckleton, 2005 pp. 464–469 for a discussion). There is a general consensus that the strength of the evidence of a match to an individual on the NDNAD is not affected by the fact that the search was carried out in the first place. Buckleton summarizes: "the evidence is always stronger after a database search and reporting the standard LR is always conservative." Recall Eqn 4.9, assume $w_{i,s} = 1$:

$$P(G|E_{dna}, E_o) = \frac{1}{1 + (N - 1)R_{i,s}} \tag{4.12}$$

In a database search, a proportion of individuals are eliminated from the inquiry because the DNA profile does not match. Therefore, if M people are eliminated, then the size of the target population is reduced. Because the number of possible contributors decreases, this in turn increases the strength of evidence hence the probability in Eqn 4.13 is always greater than that derived from Eqn 4.12 simply because the size of the unknown target population is reduced.

$$P(G|E_{dna}, E_o) = \frac{1}{1 + (N - M - 1)R_{i,s}} \tag{4.13}$$

To illustrate with the Narborough example (ignoring the original misidentification), all 5000 individuals were typed from the target population and 4999 were eliminated, leaving just one individual with a matching DNA profile (with match probability of 5×10^{-8}) (Gill and Werrett, 1987), hence:

$$P(G|E_{dna}, E_o) = \frac{1}{1 + (5000 - 4999 - 1) \times 5 \times 10^{-8}}$$

$$P(G|E_{dna}, E_o) = \frac{1}{1 + 0} \tag{4.14}$$

If all individuals within the population containing the perpetrator are correctly eliminated, so that only one remains, then the strength of evidence in support of the prosecution hypothesis approaches certainty.

However, in a typical database search, this is not realistic; only a proportion of individuals are eliminated from a target population.

The calculation (Eqn 4.13) is strictly conditioned upon the size of the target population (N) and the number of individuals in the database of the relevant geographic area (M). The raw LR $(1/R_{i,s})^5$ or match probability ($R_{i,s}$) is itself unchanged as it is not dependent on either of the two parameters. Assuming the other evidence is neutral, the strength of evidence expressed as odds$(G)^6$ alters according to the size of the unknown population that is expressed by $N - M$ (Table 4.2).

In terms of the posterior probability (or odds) of guilt, it is only the size of the *unknown* target population that is defined by $N - M$ that is relevant to the calculation. The size of the target population may indeed be reduced by database searches, but the most effective method is to restrict the target population itself as described in Section 4.18. If the calculation does not incorporate the target population parameter (N), then the raw LR $1/R_{i,s} = 2 \times 10^7$, that is reported in current practice, is always much larger than any of the population adjusted figures after conversion to odds(G). The LR and odds converge numerically when $N - M = 2$.

In practice, a court will be handed a raw statistic, which by itself appears to be compelling evidence. Of course there will be warnings made by the

Table 4.2 A Suspect Is Identified with a DNA Likelihood Ratio $1/R_{i,s} = 2 \times 10^7$ and This Is the Raw Statistic That Is Provided to the Court

Target population size (N-M)	$P(G|E)$	Odds(G)
1	1.00000E + 00	
2	1.00000E + 00	2.00E + 07
10	1.00000E + 00	2.22E + 06
100	9.99995E − 01	2.02E + 05
1000	9.99950E − 01	2.00E + 04
10,000	9.99500E − 01	2.00E + 03

The target population size N is reduced by the database search or dragnet to N–M individuals. The strength of evidence depends upon the size of N–M. 'E' is a notation used in Excel that stands for times 10 raised to a power indicated to the right of the expression.

---

[5] The reciprocal is used so that the LR is consistent with previous chapters: the numerator evaluates the prosecution hypothesis and the denominator evaluates the defense hypothesis.

[6] Probabilities are converted to odds ($p/1 - p$) since it is difficult to "visualize" probabilities that are recurring 0.9999.

scientist to avoid the prosecutor's fallacy. The statistic provided by the LR is strictly conditioned upon $Pr(E|G)$, but a court cannot convict an individual unless it can evaluate $Pr(G|E)$ in the context of the target population and/or the non-DNA evidence. Courts work in an intuitive way, but it is difficult to see how the DNA statistic can be placed into perspective without the formal approach outlined. There is nothing new here. Similar suggestions have been made by Meester and Sjerps (2003, 2004). A way forward is proposed by Buckleton et al. (2006) that involves use of Bayes net solutions.

4.20 APPEAL-COURT RULINGS ON THE USE OF BAYES THEOREM

The appeal court in R. v. Adams rejected the idea of a full Bayesian analysis of the data—it was clearly struggling with the concept but nevertheless appeared to agree that it was important to provide guidance to a jury about the relevant population to consider along with the number of individuals that could have contributed to the crime-stain sample. Here the emphasis of this chapter is to introduce the concepts to the investigator, where the only barrier is education. But this would seem to be a necessary precursor before the concepts can be reintroduced to courts.

4.21 HOW FAR HAVE THE COURTS ADOPTED THIS THINKING?

The issue with the Adams case was that there was significant exculpatory evidence and the DNA was consequently the only primary evidence offered (a typical *type II* case from a database search):

• The victim failed to identify the suspect in a "line-up."
• The victim stated that the defendant did not look like the man who attacked her and he did not fit the description that she gave of her attacker. She stated that he appeared to be older than her attacker.
• Adams stated that he had spent the entire evening with his girlfriend during the time of the attack and the alibi witness was not discredited.

The prosecution and defense scientists collaborated with each other to provide a questionnaire for the jury to fill in the answers to the probabilities to questions such as:

1. What is the chance, assuming nothing else about the case, that the rapist came from the local area?
2. What is the chance that the victim would fail to identify Adams?

3. What is the chance of the defendant's evidence?
4. What is the chance of the alibi evidence?

The proposal was put forward that once the probabilities had been decided and agreed by the jury, then they would determine a posterior probability of guilt. In order to provide the jury with examples, Professor Donnelly explained the process with "what-if" examples, and it was stressed that it was up to the jury to decide which probabilities to apply.

Despite the efforts of the defense argument, Adams was found to be guilty, and the case went to appeal again and yet another retrial was granted. In the judgment it was stated:

> ... we have very grave doubt as to whether that evidence [using Bayes theorem] was properly admissible, because it trespasses on an area peculiarly and exclusively within the province of the jury, namely the way in which they evaluate the relationship between one piece of evidence and another.

Therefore, it appears that there was a fundamental "legal" constraint on the way that the evidence was combined.

> the apparently objective numerical figures used in the theorem may conceal the element of judgment on which it entirely depends.
> More fundamentally, however, the mathematical formula, applied to each separate piece of evidence, is simply inappropriate to the jury's task. Jurors evaluate evidence and reach a conclusion not only by means of a formula, mathematical or otherwise, but by the joint application of their individual common sense and knowledge of the world to the evidence before them.

Comment: The jury is presented with a large LR from the DNA evidence and expected to place it into the context of the non-numeric, non-DNA evidence using "common sense." However, intuitive processes are subject to innate cognitive errors—see Section 4.17.

Once the arguments had been put to the second appeal court (1997) the judgment stated:

> quantification was appropriate for the prosecution's DNA evidence, in so far as that evidence was based ... on empirical statistical data, the data and the deductions drawn from it being available for the defense to criticize and challenge. The Court characterized the defense's evidence as non-scientific, non-DNA evidence and rejected the argument that such evidence should be represented in statistical form.

Therefore, the complaint of the judges was directed toward the attempt to quantify non-scientific evidence. This was entirely understandable. It is unreasonable to expect juries or scientists to formulate probabilities based on matters where there are no data. There are no data to inform questions such as:

- "If he were the attacker, what's the chance that she would say he looked nothing like the attacker?"
- "If he was not the attacker what's the chance that she would say he looked nothing like the attacker?"

The following is a quote from Lynch and McNally (2003):

> *In sum, the two* Adams *appeal-court decisions characterized the Bayesian approach as an individualistic, reductive calculus that creates a misleading or potentially confusing appearance of objectivity when applied to non-scientific evidence.*

- To summarize it was not the use of Bayes theorem *per se* that the court rejected—rather the problem was the suggestion that probabilistic methods could be used where there was no possibility of providing meaningful probabilities to the questions posed.
- If the discussion had focussed solely on the scientific method to apply meaningful probabilities from geographic profiling evidence, in order to restrict the target population size, then this could have been combined with the DNA evidence in the manner proposed by Donnelly, using methods described here.
- Finally, there is no barrier for the investigator to implement the thinking described in this chapter. This is needed in order to prevent cognitive biases being inadvertently propagated to courts by experts.

4.21.1 Court of Appeal Agreement with the Concept of the Target Population

The idea of a target population is not controversial in the appeal of *Regina v. Doheny and Adams* 1997 (note this is a different "Adams" to the previous one).

> *Provided that the expert has the necessary data, it may then be appropriate for the expert to indicate how many people with the matching characteristics are likely to be found in the (United Kingdom) or a more limited relevant sub-group, for instance, the Caucasian, sexually active males in the (Manchester area). It is then for the jury to decide, having regard to all the relevant evidence,*

whether they are sure that it was the defendant who left the crime stain or whether it is possible it was left by someone else with the same matching DNA characteristics.

Cautiously worded, the scientist was invited to assist the court to place the evidence into context of a population. Note that there have been various criticisms of the approach—for example, the issue of relatedness is not covered—but this is largely irrelevant since these factors can easily be accommodated with new calculations if required (Balding, 2005, pp. 111–134).

The Forensic Science Service duly supported the court recommendation with R. v. Wilkinson (Unreported, Leeds Crown Court). In this case the crime-stain profile was highly degraded, hence there was a relatively high probability of a random match. In discussion with both the defense and prosecution lawyers, it was agreed to present the statistical analysis in the context of census population sizes as shown in Table 4.3. The idea was to present the data in the context of a target population size. This was the limit of the analysis carried out. It was left to the court to decide the meaning of the evidence, but of course it is a simple step to formulate prior probabilities as described in previous sections.

In the R. v. Doheny and Adams case, both prosecution and defense agreed that the perpetrator was from a population consisting of 800,000 people, living in the area of Manchester. The DNA profiling evidence combined with conventional blood grouping concluded a LR of 40,000, called by the judges the *random occurrence ratio* of 1 in 40,000. The term *random occurrence ratio* is taken to mean the chance of observing a profile in random set of (unrelated) people—a match probability. The judges recommended that it should be explained to a jury in terms of the number

Table 4.3 Presentation of Data in R. v. Wilkinson (Note That the Expectations Are Based on Average Estimates)	
Number of men (rounded to the nearest 1000)	Expected number of men with matching characteristics
30,000,000	867
1,219,000	37
46,000	2[a]
[a] Rounded up from 1.4.	

of individuals in the target population of 800,000 who would possess the "relevant characteristics." In this example there could be 20 other people with the same DNA profile. The judges concluded that *this figure still renders it an extremely unlikely coincidence that both the Appellant and another of this small cohort should have been in the vicinity of the crime at about the same time that it was committed.*

Analyzing the data using the strength of evidence method given previously (for the target population) gives:

$$P(G|E_{dna}, E_o) \;=\; \frac{1}{1 + (n-1)w_{i,s=1}R_{i,s}}$$

$$P(G|E_{dna}, E_o) \;=\; \frac{1}{1 + (800,000 - 1) \times 1/40000}$$

$$P(G|E_o) \;\approx\; 0.047 \quad \text{(favoring innocence)} \qquad (4.15)$$

4.22 THE DEFENDANT'S FALLACY IS NOT NECESSARILY A FALLACY

The "defendant's fallacy" or the "defense lawyer fallacy" is frequently quoted as an error of logic and it is raised here since the previous section leads directly to its possibility in the *type II* case example. Continuing with the above example: the fallacy would argue that since the expected number of people in the target population is 800,000 and the profile frequency is 1/40,000; given the probability that the defendant is the culprit is 0.047 (from the equation above) we expect there to be approximately $1/0.047 \approx 20$(unknown) people with the same profile characteristics. However, the statement is valid under certain circumstances (Balding, 2005, p. 147):

• The background population has been filtered so that the target population comprises individuals of the correct age group, geographical location, reduced by the database search, etc., then the first point is satisfactorily addressed.
• If a database search has been used to identify the defendant (so it is a *type II* case) and the "other evidence" is neutral then the second point is addressed. Note that if the other evidence is exculpatory then the odds of guilt are reduced further.
• Assuming the above conditions are fulfilled: the judges' conclusion in the previous case that: *this figure still renders it an extremely unlikely*

coincidence that both the Appellant and another of this small cohort should have been in the vicinity of the crime at about the same time that it was committed would itself be a fallacious argument if the suspect had been derived from a database search (*type II* case) and the other evidence was neutral or exculpatory. In which case the odds G are correctly stated as 20:1 against guilt because $w_{i,s} = 1$ and the other non-DNA evidence is neutral.

I have called the false invocation of the "defendant's fallacy," the "defendant's double fallacy."

Commentators on the defendant's fallacy have readily assumed that courts never convict unless the non-DNA evidence is probative. However, the cases discussed in this book suggest that this premise is incorrect. Unfortunately in most of the appeals discussed, the other evidence is usually limited, and may be exculpatory. The court may over-rely upon the "swamping effect" (Section 4.17) of the DNA evidence to absorb non-DNA neutral or exculpatory evidence. In the absence of the correct calculations, the effect will tend to reinforce "confirmation bias." Only a few cases ever reach the appeal stage and an unknown number are prosecuted solely on DNA evidence alone. The solution is to reconcile the non-DNA evidence with the DNA evidence, described in the following section which would avoid the need to consider whether the defendant's fallacy is relevant or not.

4.23 RECONCILING THE NON-DNA EVIDENCE WITH THE DNA EVIDENCE

To reconcile the strands of evidence, it is necessary to combine the non-DNA evidence with the DNA evidence to furnish a posterior probability. Balding (2005) discusses this on page 29 of his book using eye-witness evidence as an example to inform an addition $R_{i,s}^{other}$ calculation:

$$P(G|E_{dna}E_{other}E_o) = \frac{1}{1 + (N-1)w_{i,s}R_{i,s}^{dna}R_{i,s}^{other}} \quad (4.16)$$

Continuing with the R. v. Doheny and Adams case example where $N = 800,000$, $w_{i,s} = 1$, $R_{i,s}^{dna} = 1/40,000$, what is the level of $1/R_{i,s}^{other}$ required to be probative? A number greater than one favors the prosecution argument and a number less than one favors the defense argument.

Table 4.4 The R. v. Doheny and Adams Case—Effect of the "Other Non-DNA Evidence" on *P(G|E)* and the Corresponding Odds *(G)*

$1/R_{i,s}^{other}$	$P(G|E)$	Odds (G)
1	0.04762	0.05
10	0.33333	0.50
100	0.83333	5
1000	0.98039	50
10,000	0.99800	500
100,000	0.99980	5000
1,000,000	0.99998	50,000

$N = 800,000$, $w_{i,s} = 1$, $R_{i,s}^{dna} = 1/40,000$. As the $1/R_{i,s}^{other}$ increases, it supports the prosecution argument, the overall strength of evidence increases.

From Table 4.4, for the evidence to be neutral $P(G|E) = 1$, $1/R_{i,s}^{other} = 20$. To achieve $P(G|E) = 0.9998$ requires $1/R_{i,s}^{other} = 100,000$. In this example, the strength of the non-DNA evidence needs to be substantial in order to reach the suggested $P(G|E)$. This conclusion does not follow from intuitive thought.

This case dates back to 1997, when DNA profiling was relatively young. Today, prosecution authorities would probably be reticent to report what are regarded as "low figures," favoring 1 in 1 million as the maximum reportable match probability. Using the same parameters described for Table 4.4, substitution of the DNA profiling match probability of 1/40,000 with 1/1 million and 1/1 billion transforms the probabilistic assessment (Table 4.5).

The 1 in 1 billion concept applied to SGM Plus is sometimes applied as an artificial reporting threshold. The actual match probability is in the region of 1 in 10^{13} and the new multiplexes have a much greater power to discriminate, typically 1 in 10^{19} for 15 locus systems. This means that very high posterior odds (G) can be achieved even if the other non-DNA evidence expressed by the LR $1/R_{i,s}^{other}$ is exculpatory (Table 4.6). Note that $1/R_{i,s}^{other} > 1$ favors the prosecution hypothesis and $1/R_{i,s}^{other} < 1$ favors the defense hypothesis.

Table 4.6 shows the effect of combining incriminating DNA evidence with exculpatory non-DNA evidence when a matching full profile is obtained with the SGM Plus system and the new multiplex systems. For example, neutrality is achieved with the SGM Plus system with a staggering:

Table 4.5 Here, the Match Probabilities of the DNA Profile Are Substantially Reduced to 1 in 1 Million and 1 in 1 Billion				
	$R_{i,s}^{dna} = 1/1$ million		$R_{i,s}^{dna} = 1/1$ billion	
$1/R_{i,s}^{other}$	P(G|E)	Odds(G)	P(G|E)	Odds(G)
1	0.56	1.25	0.99920	1250
10	0.93	12.50	0.99992	12,500
100	0.992	125	0.99999	125,000
1000	0.9992	1250	1.0	1.25E + 06
10,000	0.99992	12,500	1.0	1.25E + 07
100,000	0.999992	125,000	1.0	1.25E + 08
1,000,000	0.999999	1,250,000	1.0	1.25E + 09

The effect is that this greatly increases the P(G\|E) to the extent that if the other evidence is neutral (for the 1/1 billion example), the evidence still supports the prosecution hypothesis. Note 'E' in the odds column stands for times 10 raised to a power denoted after the expression (also used in subsequent tables)

Table 4.6 A Demonstration of the Ability of Very Low DNA Match Probabilities to "Absorb" Exculpatory DNA Evidence				
	$R_{i,s}^{dna} = 1/10E+13$		$R_{i,s}^{dna} = 1/1E+19$	
$1/R_{i,s}^{other}$	P(G|E)	Odds(G)	P(G|E)	Odds(G)
1E−09	0.01235	0.01	0.99920	1250
1E−08	0.11111	0.13	0.99992	12,500
1E−07	0.55556	1	0.99999	125,000
1E−06	0.92593	13	1.0	1.25E + 06
1E−05	0.99206	125	1.0	1.25E + 07
0.0001	0.99920	1250	1.0	1.25E + 08
0.001	0.99992	12,500	1.0	1.25E + 09

$1/R_{i,s}^{other} = 1/10$ million (in support of the defense hypothesis). The new multiplex systems have a phenomenal power to "absorb" evidence that may support the defense hypothesis.

4.24 THE FALSE POSITIVE ERROR (THE ELEPHANT IN THE ROOM)

The preceding section has assumed throughout that the DNA profile was error-free but this is unrealistic. The wrongful arrest of Adam Scott was a classic example of the false positive error, where a contamination incident affected a crime sample (Chapter 2). An example where the probative value of the DNA evidence was very powerful, tending to mitigate the contrary defense evidence.

Balding (2005, p. 16) describes the effect of "typing errors":

the overall weight of the evidence involves adding together the probability of a chance match and the probability of a match due to a typing error

Taking the case of Adam Scott where the match probability was based on population frequency estimates and described as 1 in 1 billion: the typing error was shown to be a problem of laboratory contamination from an earlier incident where the samples were processed. Error rates are not used in any laboratory, so it is necessary to introduce a proxy. Suppose the chance of an error rate is one in approximately 10,000 (based on Scott). If a very convincing $R_{i,s}^{dna} = 10^{-19}$ is calculated but the false positive error rate $FPP = 10^{-4}$ then it is necessary to adjust $R_{i,s}^{dna} + FPP \approx 10^{-4}$.

- Opponents of using error rates will readily point out that they cannot be easily measured and they are difficult to categorize. This may be true, but this is not a reason to "do nothing." Here the idea of using a proxy measurement is proposed that is based upon laboratory data. A proactive approach to error measurement is preferred.
- If the error rate is greater than the probability of the population estimate of the match probability, then the adjusted match probability defaults to the error rate: $R_{i,s}^{dna} \approx FPP$.

From Thompson et al. (2003):

$$R_{i,s}^{dna} = p + [FPP \times (1 - p)] \qquad (4.17)$$

where p is the DNA match probability and FPP is the false positive probability (of the DNA match).

4.25 PUTTING IT ALL TOGETHER: A SIMPLE METHOD FOR THE INVESTIGATOR TO FOLLOW

It is possible to combine the probability of a chance match, the probability of an error, the probability of the other non-DNA evidence and the size of the "target population." The formula is simplified to consider a target population where the individuals are deemed equally likely to be guilty of the crime hence $w_{i,s} = 1$, noting that the outside population did not have a great effect on the outcome. However, the basic formula can easily be expanded to accommodate any scenario—e.g., different populations, relatives, etc. The first step is for investigators to use the methods routinely.

$$P(G|E_{dna}E_{FPP}E_{other}E_o) \approx \frac{1}{1 + N(R_{i,s}^{dna} + FPP)R_{i,s}^{other}} \qquad (4.18)$$

The combined analysis can be obtained from a simple spreadsheet (Table 4.7).

1. In practice, the court is only presented with the findings in row one, i.e., the probability that is based upon the DNA evidence itself. There has been much debate about the method used to calculate this statistic and much research effort has been devoted to its fine tuning by the application of adjustment statistics, such as estimates of relatedness. However, considerations of error rates, target population size, and strength of the other non-DNA evidence tend to have much greater effects on the combined strength of evidence.
2. The suspect will come from a relevant target population of individuals that could have committed the crime. Here we consider a population of 50,000. This has little effect in terms of $P(G|E)$. The corresponding posterior odds (G) are reduced to 20,000:1.

Table 4.7 Examples Showing How the $P(G|E)$ and the Corresponding Odds (G) Are Affected by the Assumptions of N, the Other Non-DNA Evidence and the Error Rate

		Input parameters			Output	
Comment	N	$1/R_{i,s}^{dna}$	$1/R_{i,s}^{other}$	$1/error$	$P(G|E)$	Odds(G)
The classic starting position (only DNA evidence is considered)	1	1.00E+09	1	0	1.00000	1.00E+09
Factor a target population of 50,000, other evidence is neutral	50,000	1.00E+09	1	0	0.99995	20,000
There is other evidence to implicate the suspect	50,000	1.00E+09	100	0	1.00000	2.00E+06
There is an error rate of one in 100,000	50,000	1.00E+09	100	100,000	0.99502	199.98
The other evidence is neutral	50,000	1.00E+09	1	100,000	0.66664	2.00
The other evidence is exculpatory	50,000	1.00E+09	0.01	100,000	0.01961	0.02

3. Provided that there is probative non-DNA evidence (here we assume 1 in 100 favoring the prosecution hypothesis) then $P(G|E)$ increases and the odds(G) are 2 million:1.
4. Now factor an error rate of 1 in 100,000 . The evidence is still probative $P(G|E) = 0.995$ and the odds $G = 200 : 1$.
5. If the non-DNA evidence against the suspect is neutral or exculpatory then the evidence is weak $P(G|E) = 2.0$ or supports the defense hypothesis $P(G|E) = 0.02$.

The illustration enables a deeper understanding of how miscarriages of justice, such as the wrongful arrest of Adam Scott can occur. The error rates, the exculpatory evidence, and size of the target population were not initially considered in this case; only the fact of the DNA profile was reported. Once the error was discovered, rather than declare an error rate, the event was dismissed as a "one-off," no other errors were discovered and therefore it was assumed that they do not exist. However, this is a prime example of institutional "confirmation bias" (absence of evidence is not evidence of absence).

It may be argued that it is the court's responsibility to assess the meaning of the evidence in relation to the other evidence in the case. It may also be argued that scientists should follow directions from courts regarding the scientific methods to be used. However, the above demonstrations show that the evaluation is not an intuitive exercise that is within the realms of "everyday experience" of the jury. It is difficult to understand how a court can reach logical conclusions in the absence of probabilistic assessments. Ignoring the error rates, the target population and the non-DNA evidence in a case can be strongly prosecution biased.

4.26 CONCLUSION

- Simply handing a court a LR or a match probability and expecting the statistic to be used to place the evidence into context of the other evidence using an intuitive process is not realistic (especially if the information relating to error rates is not considered).
- A compensatory method has evolved that focuses on the extreme discriminating power of the DNA profile in the hope that the number "swamps" the uncertainty that may arise from exculpatory evidence. Although there have been many warnings on the interpretation of DNA evidence—in particular the prosecutor's fallacy (Balding and Donnelly, 1994) warns that the evidence must be considered conditioned on the

innocence/guilt of an individual $P(E|G)$—this is only a small part of the overall consideration. The DNA evidence has to be interpreted in context of the target population size, the error rates and the strength of the non-DNA evidence.

- The fact of the DNA database search increases the chances of wrongful conviction since the *type II* case typically relies upon the DNA profile as primary evidence to convict. In the absence of scientific guidance, "confirmation bias" can override the other evidence in the case if it is neutral or exculpatory. The defendant's fallacy is not a fallacy if the DNA evidence is "sole-plank" and the other non-DNA evidence is neutral.

4.27 THE WAY FORWARD?

The decision to prosecute an individual is the responsibility of the prosecution authorities (the Crown Prosecution Service in England and Wales). Prosecutions are only carried out if the authorities believe that there is a realistic chance of a successful outcome. It follows that to be able to make a decision that is based on DNA profiling; it is necessary for investigators to be cognisant of the methods described in this chapter summarized as follows:

Recommendation 11:

1. Much more emphasis to be placed upon error rate discovery—that is, proactive involvement of regulatory authorities is needed—blind trials need to be propagated.
2. In the absence of an error rate, a proxy (nonzero) error rate(s) needs serious consideration.

Recommendation 12:

1. Investigators to be trained to carry out "strength of evidence calculations" that combine DNA with non-DNA evidence using a Bayesian framework. A simple demonstration is provided in Section 4.25 where the basic formula is provided.
2. The "other (non-DNA) evidence" in a case should be evaluated. What numeric level of "other-evidence" is required in order for the totality of evidence to be probative?
3. Use of geographic profiling is useful to inform the size of the target population and to refine the weights applied to Bayesian calculations.
4. Training required to ensure that investigators are aware of cognitive biases and are able to recognize the effects.

4.28 COMPLEX DNA PROFILES: THE WORRYING CASE OF R. v. DLUGOSZ—AN EXAMPLE OF A DUBIOUS APPEAL-COURT DECISION

So far, I have only considered the analysis of simple crime stains that have originated from a single contributor. The extension to complex DNA profiles is not straightforward. It is not possible to apply simple match probabilities to these calculations, it is necessary to use a LR approach but this is accommodated within the framework described previously. There has been significant progress recently to design new probabilistic methods to interpret complex mixtures (Balding and Buckleton, 2009; Bright et al., 2014; Haned and Gill, 2011; Perlin and Sinelnikov, 2009), and they are beginning to be implemented in laboratories worldwide (Prieto et al., 2014). In the case described in the following section, a retrograde method of reporting that relies upon the "experience" of experts is described.

4.29 R. v. DLUGOSZ

The only forensic evidence in the exemplar case under consideration was "very small quantities of DNA" found on two chisels used to enter a premises. The results were interpreted as mixed low template profiles and the suspect (Dlugosz) was identified by database trawl using a commercial computer program (DNABoost^{TM}) (Pope et al., 2009). No details have been publicly released about the validation, hence this is the first external peer review. It is based upon a matching allele count (MAC) method where the number of alleles present in the case stain is matched to a reference sample trawled from the UK NDNAD.[7] In the appeal-court ruling (*Regina v. Dlugosz*, 2013) it was acknowledged that without the DNA evidence, little would remain that could be used to safely convict. The court also stated that the method used to identify suspects was irrelevant, and it was not disclosed to the jury.

4.30 CAN EXPERT OPINION REPLACE PEER REVIEW?

The primary focus of the appeal was to determine whether it was possible for scientists to provide a generalized "expert opinion" based solely upon

---

[7]A reference profile on the database has a maximum of 20 alleles. The program searches for full and near matches so that they may be ranked in order: 20,19,18,17, and the theory is that the true donor is more likely to have a high number of matching alleles.

a background of "personal experience." A proposal to use a LR evaluation at trial was rejected as "unvalidated." However, it was successfully argued by the prosecution that "scientific evidence" could be based on personal experience and observations of "thousands" of cases reported, where many were mixtures. The prosecution said:

> she had not seen all 20 of the components of an individual's profile represented in a mixed profile when it was believed that the individual had no association with the item from which the profile was obtained.

The reader will note the specific wording used is: *when it was believed that the individual had no association*—the difficulty here from the scientific perspective is that the word "belief" does not correspond with any verifiable truth state. The "observations" of the scientist were based upon casework so there was no way of knowing definitively if the matches were from a defendant or not.

> When she had compared the STR profile of a completely random individual to a mixed profile, she had never observed all 20 components matching by chance

Again, this statement was part of the *belief* of the scientist. The defense challenged the opinion on the entirely reasonable basis that no data were presented, but despite displaying some initial doubt, the final conclusion of the judges was:

> the view of the experts on DNA that finding all of an individual's alleles in a mixed sample of the kind analyzed in this case was either "rare" or "somewhat unusual", was of real assistance.

In the case of MDS,[8] there was a low stringency match of 14 out of 20 alleles confirmed as matching the crime stain (6 were unconfirmed). The prosecution scientist reported:

> It is therefore my opinion that the results provide moderate support for the view that MDS has contributed DNA to this sample rather than the view he has not.

To conclude, the judges found that it was reasonable for a scientist to express a view about the probative value of complex DNA low-level mixtures,

---

[8]This is a reference to an individual who cannot be identified for legal reasons.

where most (but not necessarily all) of the alleles matched a defendant. The match may be derived from a search of the NDNAD. This conclusion was highly disconcerting because it placed the opinion or *beliefs* of the scientist above the requirement to follow the *scientific method* that requires data, analysis, and peer review in order to verify any conclusion.

4.31 A REMINDER OF THE "SCIENTIFIC METHOD"

A brief reminder of the "scientific method" is provided here since it is fundamental to the way that a court (or anyone else) should consider the validity of scientific evidence.

The modern scientific method was established several centuries ago and we can trace its origins to Galileo and Newton. It is succinctly defined by the Oxford English Dictionary as: "*a method or procedure that has characterized natural science since the 17th century, consisting in systematic observation, measurement, and experiment, and the formulation, testing, and modification of hypotheses.*"

The essentials are:

1. The hypothesis is constructed from *belief* of some principle.
2. The hypothesis is tested by experiment and a body of data is generated to support the *belief*.
3. Peer review is carried out to verify the procedure and the *belief* may be modified accordingly.

In the cases described, the hypothesis has been formulated according to a belief which can be summarized: "*It is rare for alleles to match a random non-contributor when a complex (partial) crime stain comprised of multiple individuals is considered.*" The belief was qualified by "personal observations," unsubstantiated by any data collection from known control experiments or data analysis. There was no published peer-reviewed evaluation of the methods employed, neither was the implication of automated (MAC) database searching of NDNADs using the DNAboost^{TM} method considered.

Therefore, the procedures heard in court could easily be challenged on the basis that they did not follow the universally recognized principles of the *scientific method* since steps (2) and (3), listed above, were clearly missing.

4.32 FALSE POSITIVE RESULTS

This chapter has focused primarily on the full (unambiguous) single contributor DNA profiles and for this category of sample, false positives are very rare since the probability of a chance match with the SGM Plus genotype average is 10^{-13} (Butler, 2011). For the partial *single* contributor DNA profile, the probability increases as the level of drop-out increases (Hicks et al., 2010a,b). It was shown in Section 2.7.4, for the full DNA profile, the more contributors to a crime stain, the more likely it is that a false positive match will occur. Random match probabilities are more likely with low-template DNA profiles that are multi-contributor mixtures. False positives can occur as a result of "composite results" from two or more contributors (Bleka et al., 2013; Bright et al., 2014) illustrated in Figure 4.5.

An expression of the "rarity of the DNA profile" tells the court nothing about strength of evidence in relation to a named individual who happens to match. If the true donor resides on the database but has several dropped-out alleles (Figure 4.5) then he may be undetected, resulting in a false negative (exclusion).

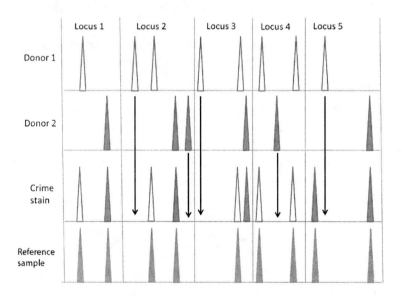

Figure 4.5 Suppose that a low-template crime stain is composed of two donors (Donor 1 and Donor 2). Since drop-out of both has occurred (represented by the arrows), neither are fully represented in the crime stain (third panel). Donor 1 has three missing alleles and Donor 2 has two missing alleles. The match illustrated in the Reference sample is with a sample on the database and it is a composite, false positive, result of the combined alleles of Donor 1 and Donor 2. Since some of the Donor 1 and Donor 2 alleles are missing, even if present as true donors in the database, they may be eliminated from an investigation as false negative results.

Whereas it is true that a two person full DNA profile has low probability of matching an individual on the database, the extension to *multiple* contributors: three (or more) person low-template mixtures requires a much deeper analysis.

To make matters worse, the court ruling in *Regina v. Dlugosz* (2013) dismissed the scientific implications of the search method as irrelevant:

> *The police used a computer program known as DNABoost™ through which they identified two persons who might match the profiles obtained. One was Dlugosz. This was used solely for the investigation. It was not relied on as evidence and can be ignored.*

However, here the converse is argued. Within the context of the database search, the chance of observing false positive matches cannot be described as "rare." If DNA evidence is the major or sole plank in an investigation, the danger is that database matches are simply selected by the naïve investigator for prosecution without a proper consideration of exculpatory evidence. Confirmation bias takes over. The issue is whether the "observation" of a rare event based on experience alone can be useful to safely adduce strength of evidence within the context of a database search? What is the chance of identifying the wrong person (a false positive error)? Of additional public concern we ask: What is the chance of wrongly eliminating a true perpetrator (false negative error)?

The questions were examined experimentally (Gill et al., 2014) as follows: To prepare a database similar in size to that held by the United Kingdom, a total of $N = 5$ million SGM Plus DNA genotypes were simulated and a simulated defendant reference $(N + 1)$ genotype was included as the test sample. The results were evaluated with the *ad hoc* (MAC) allele counting method and were compared directly using an established probabilistic method: "LRmix" (Haned, 2011) to calculate LRs for each of the $N + 1$ genotypes. It was stated by the court of appeal that the mixtures analyzed were from "at least three and two people," respectively, for the crime stains BRW(1/3) and BRW(1/4), these assumptions were defaults in the simulations.

The data were sorted into descending order of the LRs and the number of matching alleles present were simultaneously recorded for each of the two crime-stain profiles. An example is shown in Figure 4.6.

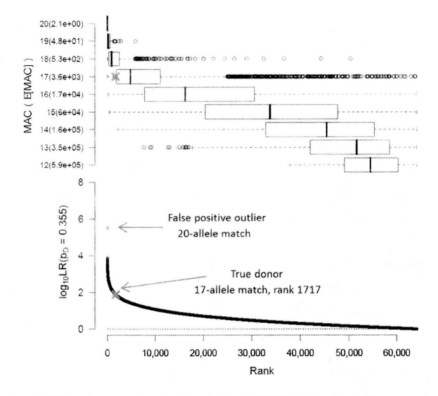

Figure 4.6 This is a three-person mixture simulation of crime-stain BRW(1/3). It is based on the Dlugosz case using simulated profiles that are defined by the characteristics of the case in terms of numbers of contributors (three) and the estimated allele drop-out rate.

For traditional database searches (not familial searches) precisely one match is expected with LR $\gg$ 1 if the donor is present (and there is a full DNA profile). Mathematically, the $N - 1$ exclusions (where LR $\ll$ 1) strengthens the LR match (Section 4.19).

The concept of match or non-match, usually assumed by previous commentators, does not apply to complex DNA profiles (Gill and Buckleton, 2010). However, advanced methods of interpretation are able to calculate the LRs for all samples, regardless of how well they are perceived to match a reference using standard criteria. If a comparison has limited strength of evidence that suggests exclusion, it will provide a LR statistic less than 1. In Figure 4.6, the strength of the DNA evidence of the top 60,000 individuals selected from a total of 5 million individuals from a simulated NDNAD is shown in the lower panel. This is compared with the MAC method (which was the Dlugosz appeal, court-recommended method) in the upper panel.

Here the number of matching alleles 20,19,18... is shown on the *y*-axis label, together with the expected number of matches in parentheses. For example, with 19 alleles a total of 4.8 chance matches are expected when searched against a database of 5 million individuals. Box whisker plots[9] show the distribution of MACs. The position of the true donor is shown as the red cross (dark gray in print versions). Notice that the strength of evidence is low in the example shown. Furthermore, in a database search it ranks number 1717 and there are only 17 matching alleles. Conversely, a match is observed with 20 alleles with a random person held on the database. This particular sample is a clear outlier—it also has the highest LR, and it is easy to surmise that it could be wrongly chosen by the naïve investigator for prosecution. There would be a simultaneous false negative exclusion since the true donor only has 17 alleles.

Searches of databases can reveal thousands of individuals where LR > 1 (Figure 4.6). It has been shown by Gill et al. (2014) that this kind of result is typical when low-template mixtures are analyzed—i.e., a few 20 allele matches are detected from a database trawl, but they will tend to be false positive results. The true donor, if present on the database, may be hidden if his alleles have dropped out, meaning fewer alleles will match the crime stain, and he will be eliminated from the inquiry as a result.

To conclude, the MAC method cannot be generalized, as implied by the Dlugosz court ruling, to simple allele-matching criteria and it has been demonstrated that it is likely to give rise to very misleading conclusions. The observation of a majority match with a crime stain cannot be described as universally "rare."

4.33 CONCLUSION

1. The DNA database search is exploratory and its use is focussed more toward aiding investigations by creating sequential ranked lists of suspects to be evaluated by the method described in Section 4.32.
2. Generalizations based on the MAC method are ineffective. The method cannot be employed to provide an expression about the strength of

---

[9]The rectangular box of the box whisker plot contains 50% of the observations with the median shown by the vertical line in the middle. The whiskers either side of the box show the majority of the other observations and the circles are outliers that extend the entire range.

evidence in relation to any particular suspect. There is no real alternative to carrying out probabilistic calculations.

3. The unfortunate precedent set in R. v. Dlugosz is a prime example showing how the legal system can unwittingly be complicit in propagating a method that has no scientific basis. It is particularly dangerous, since the MAC method invites confirmation bias. As this is now established practice, the same errors will be repeated across different cases, illustrating the "serial-error effect." At the time of writing, the regulatory/accreditation authorities have not yet recognized the problem.

CHAPTER 5

Concluding Remarks: Illustrated by the Case of the Death of Meridith Kercher

5.1 THE DYNAMIC BACKGROUND DNA ENVIRONMENT

High prevalence of background "trace-DNA" was shown by Toothman et al. (2008) in dust samples taken from rooms of an academic institution with varying amounts of thoroughfare. Mixtures were common. There was no attempt to identify the origins of the DNA profiles in this work, but it was sufficient to establish the principle that significant background DNA exists in any human-habited environment, and pre-exists the crime scene. There are two different transfer mechanisms discussed in Section 1.3. "Active" transfer is associated with the crime event itself and involves transfer of DNA from perpetrator, or victim, to a surface, object, or person. The transfer method is either direct (by touching) or by aerosol (saliva spray from speaking or exhaling). "Passive" transfer is innocent transfer of DNA achieved by direct means; indirect (secondary transfer) or by aerosol (including shed skin cells which form house dust). See reviews by Meakin and Jamieson (2013) and van Oorschot et al. (2010) for further discussion. Current evidence suggests that direct or indirect, rather than aerosol transfer is the predominant means of contamination (Vandewoestyne et al., 2011; Witt et al., 2009); "passive" DNA transfer has been demonstrated between different items that are packaged together (Goray et al., 2012a), hence "cold cases" predating sensitive DNA analysis may be particularly prone to this kind of cross contamination. More work is needed since most of the previous studies have been carried out using older "less sensitive" multiplex systems. The position might be different with the new "ultrasensitive" systems now employed, hence an open mind is required. Certainly, the more sensitive the detection method, the higher the prevalence of background DNA becomes. It seems pre-requisite, therefore, to evaluate the pre-existing background levels at a given crime scene environment.

5.2 LABORATORY ENVIRONMENTAL MONITORING

As part of the anti-contamination control procedures of any DNA profiling laboratory, protective clothing is worn in order to mitigate the possibility of analysts accidentally cross transferring their DNA to casework samples. Visitors to laboratory facilities are required to provide a DNA profile.

However, despite best efforts, DNA profiles will always be observed in the laboratory environment and this poses a serious danger to the inadvertent cross contamination of items.

This is why environmental monitoring should be routinely carried out to assess prevailing levels of DNA—two categories of DNA profiles are present: (a) from laboratory workers and (b) unknown or unexplained profiles. The defunct FSS laboratory used to carry out routine environmental monitoring routinely. If levels were too high then the laboratory would

Table 5.1 *From Table 1 of Vandewoestyne et al. (2011)*—Numbers of Alleles Detected on Surfaces and Equipment (Before Decontamination Procedure)

Surface/equipment	RFU ≥ 100	RFU ≥ 50
Drawer of laboratory cupboard (outside surface)	10	17
Laboratory bench	12	19
Centrifuge used for reference samples (inside surface)	1	5
Centrifuge used for evidence samples (inside surface)	1	1
Container with autoclaved tubes (outside surface)	0	1
Pipetholder in laminar flow cabinet	0	1
On/off button laminar flow cabinet	7	9
Container with autoclaved filter tips	0	0
Handle laboratory freezer	7	13
Handle laboratory fridge	2	7
Box containing centrifugal filter devices (outside surface)	1	5
Rack for tubes (empty)	14	18
Vortex	3	7
Electronic pipette	5	10
Outside laminar flow cabinet (front side)	0	0
Inside laminar flow cabinet (bottom)	0	0
Inside pipetting liquid handler with UV lamp (left side)	0	0
Inside pipetting liquid handler with UV lamp (right side)	0	0
Inside pipetting liquid handler with UV lamp (bottom)	0	0

(Number of alleles detected spans RFU ≥ 100 and RFU ≥ 50 columns.)

be temporarily closed for decontamination. Vandewoestyne et al. (2011) showed that significant background contamination was found on laboratory equipment and fixtures such as door handles, laboratory benches, and drawers (Table 5.1). Levels are reduced after decontamination, but not entirely eliminated:

It can be concluded that complete decontamination of equipment and surfaces from DNA and DNA containing biological material is important in forensic DNA laboratories in order to avoid secondary transfer of this contaminating DNA to evidence samples.

It follows that stringent requirements are needed to ensure that different items of evidence are *separately* packaged and transported to a laboratory. It is also necessary to examine items from the same case in separate laboratory facilities in order to preclude the possibility of cross transfer between them.

There will be a problem with old "cold-cases" that have been analyzed several times in the past. Each time a case is examined, there is a risk of cross transfer. It is unlikely that the necessary assurances can be provided where cases have been examined several times in an environment that lacks stringent controls and the necessary documentation is absent.

Direct and indirect (secondary) transfer occurs within the controlled laboratory environment. The same processes must occur at the uncontrolled crime-scene environment, before and after the crime event itself. Of course it is not possible to decontaminate the crime scene as it would destroy any evidence, hence the levels of background contamination that are detected will be much greater than in the laboratory—the problem will be to distinguish between background contamination vs. crime-event transfer, and often this will not be possible.

Recommendation 13: To assess the background levels of DNA present in the laboratory, environmental monitoring is required. Continuity of case items should include documentation to show that they have been properly packaged, stored, transported, and examined in an environment that is designed to minimize the possibility of cross transfer between them. Sensitive items will need to be examined in separate facilities to preclude the possibility of cross contamination.

See Chapter 4 for a discussion on error rates.

5.3 ON THE LIMITATIONS OF THE INFORMATION THAT CAN BE USED TO ASSESS THE RELEVANCE OF DNA PROFILING EVIDENCE

1. To infer the association of a DNA profile with its cellular origin may be justified when discrete samples are analyzed, e.g., cleansed bone or hair shaft. But there is nothing implicit within the DNA profile itself that gives a definitive answer.
2. If there are large quantities (nanograms of DNA) along with a body fluid, such as blood, then the association is usually made with confidence. However, with "trace-DNA," the certainty of the association of DNA with cell type is much reduced (Section 2.5).
3. Once a DNA profile has been associated with a body-fluid, then the forensic scientist may seek to propose an "activity" such as sexual assault, if sperm is identified. However, this deduction is not implicit.

To counter the effect of confirmation bias, the starting position is to report the DNA profile at the "sub-source" level within the framework of propositions—there is no information at the "source-level" or the "activity" level implied at this stage of reporting. Gill (2001) reasoned:

Inevitably, there is a direct relationship between the quantity of DNA present and the relevance of the evidence.

and recommended the following caveats in a "statement of limitations" (Section 1.2.1):

1. Although a DNA profile has been obtained, it is not possible to identify the type of cells from which the DNA originated, neither is it possible to state *when* the cells were deposited.
2. It is not possible to make any conclusion about transfer and persistence of DNA in this case.

This advice is still pertinent (perhaps even more so since the sensitivity of the technique has increased 20-fold since 2001).

To make inferences about the "how" or "when" a DNA profile was transferred requires full evaluation of all possibilities. This is where "confirmation bias" has its greatest effect. It is best avoided by restricting expert opinion to relevant evidence that is peer reviewed, or where a body of data exists that may be properly examined and tested. Examples are provided in Chapter 3.

To summarize, in court, the forensic scientist has a clearly defined role:

1. To be neutral (favoring neither the prosecution nor the defense).
2. To be objective.
3. To state the limitations of the evidence.
4. The statement of limitations is assisted by a summary of *all* the fully inclusive possibilities.
5. If a scientist expresses some preference for a particular possibility, then it must be based upon scientific studies and the scientist must be able to refer to peer-reviewed publications.
6. Otherwise the scientist should not express a preference for any particular transfer method (see Figure 5.2).
7. Expert opinion based upon "personal experience" is particularly dangerous because in general this experience is not achieved via strictly controlled scientific methods, rather, the experience is gained via "uncontrolled" active casework. Note the erroneous conclusions of the appeal court in R. v. Dlugosz (Section 4.28) as a prime example.

8. To confine comments within the limits of expertise.
9. Forensic scientists do not decide the guilt or innocence of people, although clearly the evidence of the scientist is highly influential in court.

I now apply the principles outlined in this book to the contentious case of the "death of Meredith Kercher."

5.4 BACKGROUND TO THE CASE "DEATH OF MEREDITH KERCHER"

There are numerous Web sites about this case. Some support innocence and others support guilt of the defendants. For example, http://themurderofmeredithkercher.com/ campaigns for conviction of the defendants. For a Web site that campaigns for the acquittal of the defendants, see http://knoxdnareport.wordpress.com/. In both Web sites there are very useful links to English translations of the various judgments which the reader may ponder at leisure.

Photographs of the evidence (the knife alleged to be the murder weapon and the bra-clasp) are also made available on the Web sites along with the DNA profiles and various reports.

Chronologically the key reports are:

1. The Massei report (the judges reasoning for the original conviction). English translation at: http://themurderofmeredithkercher.com/PDF/Massei_Report.pdf.
2. Conti-Vecchiotti Report (a report by the defense experts appointed by the court) English version at: http://knoxdnareport.wordpress.com/.
3. The Hellmann report (the judges reasoning for the acquittal). English translation at: http://hellmannreport.wordpress.com/contents/.
4. The Galati-Costagliola appeal (the prosecution argument against the acquittal). English translation at: http://galatiappeal.wordpress.com/.
5. The Supreme Court of Cassation Motivation Report (judges overturn the acquittal and a retrial is ordered). Not available.

These reports were used to compile the details below. At the time of writing, the defendants have been reconvicted and we await the judges' reasoning. Too late for my book so I will comment on my Web site when available: https://sites.google.com/site/peterdgill/.

5.5 AN OUTLINE OF THE CASE CIRCUMSTANCES

The victim, Meredith Kercher shared an upper-floor flat with Amanda Knox and two Italian women in their late 1920s.

1. There were four young men that rented the flat below.
2. Sollecito was the boyfriend of Knox—she had started a relationship with him 6 days earlier.
3. Since the details regarding the location of the defendants is disputed, these are omitted since here only the DNA evidence is discussed. The aim is to determine if the DNA evidence provides support for any particular set of conclusions.
4. According to the defense: on the morning of the 2nd November, Amanda Knox returned home to shower and to change clothes. In the bathroom were small spots of blood in the sink; Meredith's bedroom door was locked. Knox returned to Sollecito's apartment and asked him to return to the cottage to check things out. Sollecito allegedly attempted to unsuccessfully force entry into Meredith's bedroom. The police were called, who forced entry into Meredith's bedroom and discovered the body. The cottage became a crime scene.
5. Rudy Guede was (and remains) convicted of the murder of Kercher—the evidence linking him to the murder is not discussed further here[1]. However, he is relevant to the prosecution case against Knox and Sollecito since it was he who alleged that he acted together with Knox and Sollecito.

Here, only the "trace-DNA" evidence that was used in the trial of Amanda Knox and Rafael Sollecito is discussed. There has been much debate about the other evidence in the trial. The purpose of the court is to combine the various parts of the evidence in order to make a decision on the guilt/innocence of the defendants. However, this is outside the scope of the following discussion.

---

[1] Extract from the Massei report: "The handprint found on a pillow in the room, on which the lifeless corpse of Meredith was found placed, turned out to have been made by Rudy Guede; the vaginal swab of the victim contained the DNA of the victim and of Rudy Guede (no sperm found); the DNA of Rudy Guede was also found on the cuff of Meredith's sweatshirt found in her room, and on a strap of the bra that she was wearing, found cutoff and stained with blood; the DNA of Rudy Guede was also found on Meredith's purse, which was also in the room that she occupied. Further biological traces of Rudy Guede were found on the toilet paper taken from the toilet of the larger bathroom."

5.6 THE KNIFE (ITEM 36)

5.6.1 Prosecution Propositions

1. Sollecito and Knox were alleged to be complicit in the crime along with Rudy Guede.
2. A murder weapon had not been discovered at or near the crime scene, therefore the weapon must have been removed.
3. A large knife (item 36) was found remote from the crime scene in a cutlery drawer in Sollecito's flat. The investigators alleged this to be the murder weapon.
4. The knife was tested for DNA and a profile matching Amanda Knox was found on the handle and a low-level profile matching Meredith Kercher was found on the blade.
5. The prosecution alleged that the DNA was transferred to the handle when Knox stabbed Kercher with the knife (and DNA from Kercher was consequently transferred to the blade).

5.6.2 Defense Alternative Propositions

1. Sollecito and Knox were not present when the crime was committed
2. The murder weapon was not the knife found in the cutlery drawer
3. The "trace-DNA" attributed to Knox on the handle was transferred during preparation of food (she prepared meals at Sollecito's apartment)
4. If the "trace-DNA" profile originates from Kercher (a) there is no evidence it originated from blood and (b) the transfer method is unknown, but could have occurred either by contamination (mishandling the evidence) or by secondary transfer (innocent transfer)

5.7 THE "TRACE-DNA" EVIDENCE

There appeared to be no *a priori* evidence that the knife selected from a cutlery drawer was the murder weapon (it was not covered with blood for example). The only reason that it was selected was because of an "investigative hunch" by a police officer. No other cutlery in the drawer was analyzed. The knife selected, Exhibit 36, appeared very clean, with nothing visible to the naked eye. Two profiles were obtained at the initial investigation:

36-A (handle of the knife): A single contributor DNA profile that matched Amanda Knox

36-B (blade of the knife): A single contributor (low-level) DNA profile that matched the victim, Meredith Kercher.

5.7.1 Comment on the Method of Analysis

There was fair criticism in the Conti-Vechiotti report of the method used to analyze the DNA profiling evidence. The profiles have since been reanalyzed using methods that can take account of the drop-in and drop-out phenomena associated with low-template DNA, using LRmix (Gill and Haned, 2013; Haned, 2011; Haned and Gill, 2011; Haned et al., 2012), using methods supported by the ISFG DNA Commission (Gill et al., 2012). In the latest analysis of a profile from the knife handle/junction of the knife blade, the Carabinieri also followed this method. New evidence submitted to the latest court inquiry: 36-I (junction of handle and blade of knife) revealed a two person mixture attributed by the prosecution to Amanda Knox and an unknown individual. http://www.amandaknox.com/wp-content/uploads/2013/07/Perizia-biologico-forense-PP-11-13-RG-AA-CAA-Firenze_31-10-2013.pdf. The following is an example of a standard method of reporting crime-stain evidence that utilizes the likelihood ratio method. The report is conditioned on the alternative propositions (under the assumption that each is true).

Two alternative propositions were considered at the sub-source level:

Either: under the prosecution hypothesis (Hp): the DNA profile is a mixture and originated from Amanda Knox and one unknown person.
Or: Under the defense hypothesis (Hd): the DNA profile is a mixture and it originated from two unknown persons.

The conclusion: The evidence is 700 million times more likely if the DNA profile originated from Amanda Knox and one unknown person than if it originated from two unknown persons.

Comment: Note that the standard report is restricted to an assessment of the DNA profiling evidence at sub-source level.

5.8 BRIEF SUMMARY OF THE OTHER "TRACE-DNA" PROFILES ON THE KNIFE

The profile attributed to Knox in item 36-A was unambiguous (single contributor). The profile attributed to the victim, Meredith Kercher, on the knife blade was very low level; many alleles were below the usual detection threshold of 50 rfu (rfu are measurement units) and I counted just six alleles above the threshold level, although those below the threshold level did not exclude Kercher. It is standard practice to include only those alleles above the threshold, in the likelihood ratio test. This profile was nevertheless at the limits of detection and originated from just a handful of cells—this is the kind of profile I would expect to observe, if it had originated from a contamination event. The DNA-trace evidence was calculated LR = 100 in favor of the prosecution hypothesis if it originated from Kercher (weak evidence).

5.9 THE BRA-CLASP (ITEM 165)

There has been an independent analysis of item 165 (bra-clasp) by Balding (2013) using LikeLTD software. The results are consistent with those reported here.

A bra-clasp was found at the crime scene. It had been physically cut from the victim during the offence. This item revealed a complex mixture. Analysis of the DNA profile by defense experts (Vecciotti-Conti report) indicated that it was not unreasonable to postulate three or more contributors. Note that a complex DNA profile does not explicitly provide the absolute number of contributors. There was a major contribution to the DNA profile from the victim (unsurprisingly) and the remaining foreign alleles were all very low level. The precise conditioning on the number of contributors is therefore difficult to determine. In this case the following propositions were tested using exactly the same format as described in the previous section:

Under Hp: The "trace-DNA" profile is a mixture of Sollecito, two unknown individuals and the victim Meredith Kercher
Under Hd: The "trace-DNA" profile is a mixture of three unknown individuals and the victim Meredith Kercher

Conclusion: The evidence is 2.59 million times more likely if the "trace-DNA" profile is a mixture of Sollecito, Kercher and two unknown individuals compared to the alternative proposition that it is a mixture of Kercher and three unknown individuals *(because Sollecito is innocent under the defense proposition he is replaced by an unknown individual in the statistical analysis under the defense argument)*.

Comment: Once again, the assessment of the strength of the evidence is at sub-source level and deliberately ignores the method of transfer.

Bearing in mind we are still evaluating the evidence at the *sub-source* level: the advantage of the LRmix analysis is that it allows "exploratory analysis" to be carried out. This means that the defense and the prosecution scientists can carry out "what-if" scenario analysis. With the example of the bra-clasp, the number of contributors was uncertain—how robust is the statistical analysis if the number of contributors is wrong? To test this, the number of contributors was increased to five individuals. Now the following propositions were compared:

Under Hp: The "trace-DNA" profile is a mixture of Sollecito, *three* unknown individuals and the victim Meredith Kercher.
Under Hd: The "trace-DNA" profile is a mixture of *four* unknown individuals and the victim Meredith Kercher.

Conclusion: The evidence is 181,500 times more likely if the DNA profile was a mixture of Sollecito, Kercher and three unknown individuals.

Comment: The evidence is still probative, although there is an order of magnitude reduction in the likelihood ratio.

5.10 HOW ROBUST IS THE ANSWER?

The strength of evidence that is generated in the form of the likelihood ratio is a standard method of reporting DNA evidence. The method directly compares the alternative scenarios that are proposed by the defense and the prosecution. In this example, the answers are relatively insensitive to postulating more unknown contributors. However, a raw likelihood ratio that is based upon complex alternative propositions does require extra qualification to ensure the calculation is robust. The following question is addressed:

What values of strength of evidence will be obtained if we replace Sollecito with a random person?

If the model is robust, it will be able to discriminate between a randomly chosen individual and a "true donor" to the mixture, because the former should give a very low "exclusionary" statistic (LR less than one). In Section 4.7, it was noted that a robust statistical method should be able to provide strength of evidence that supports the "defense hypothesis of exclusion." We evaluate the chance that a high likelihood ratio would be obtained from a random man substitution of the suspect.

The evidence that the model is robust is shown here: the calculation is carried out by replacing Sollecito with a random man (generated by computer simulation) so that the likelihood ratio that is evaluated is:

$$\mathrm{LR}_n = \frac{Pr(\mathrm{Evidence}|R_n, V, U, U)}{Pr(\mathrm{Evidence}|V, U, U, U)} \tag{5.1}$$

where R_n is a random genotype; V is the victim; and U are unknown individuals.

The analysis is repeated 1000 times—each time a different random man (R_n) is simulated before the calculation is carried out. We are naturally interested in the distribution of likelihood ratios that are observed if 1000 random men ($R_{1...1000}$) were assessed instead of Sollecito.

The results of the robustness analysis are shown in the cumulative distribution analysis in Figure 5.1.

Compare the maximum LR = 10 (random man substitution) with the result that included Sollecito where the LR = 2.59 million: there is a clear

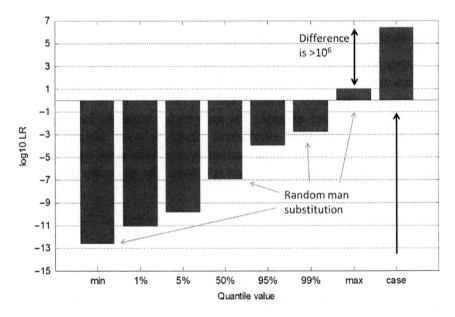

Figure 5.1 Cumulative distribution analysis of 1000 random men substituting Sollecito in the likelihood ratio calculation of the bra-clasp evidence (four person mixture), showing that the median result is very low LR = 10^{-6.9} and the maximum observed random man LR = 10. The crime-stain evidence LR = 2.59 million. The model gives very much lower LRs when interrogated with random man profiles and the difference between the case sample and maximum random man LR > 10^6.

difference in the two answers—i.e., the likelihood ratio model clearly excludes random men as potential contributors.

To conclude, from the analysis of the bra-clasp (item 165) and the knife (item 36) the evidence supports the following prosecution propositions:

1. "trace-DNA" evidence attributed to Sollecito was obtained from the bra-clasp
2. "trace-DNA" evidence attributed to Amanda Knox was obtained from the handle of the knife
3. "trace-DNA" evidence attributed to Amanda Knox was obtained from the junction of the blade and handle of the knife
4. "trace-DNA" evidence attributed to Meredith Kercher was obtained from the blade of the knife

Note that the evidence is "trace-DNA"; recall the definition in Section 1.2. So far nothing has been said about how the profiles could have been transferred to become evidential and this is key to the evaluation of the case.

5.11 FURTHER EVALUATION OF DNA PROFILING EVIDENCE: THE LIMITATIONS

In order to further evaluate evidence, we begin with the framework of propositions (already discussed in Section 1.7). The "framework of propositions" is listed below:

• Level 3—the offence level:
  – Was a crime committed by the defendant or an unrelated person?
  – The forensic scientist would rarely consider evidence at this level.
• Level 2—the activity level:
  – Did the defendant/unrelated person take part in a connected activity?
  – Substantial other evidence is needed to report at the activity level.
• Level 1—the source level:
  – The association of a DNA profile with a body fluid is not implicit. They are two separate and independent tests.
  – Scientists must have relevant background information to report above level 1.

- Sub-level 1—sub-source level:
  - Low quantity, degraded/small stains, no background information.
  - No association made between body fluid and DNA profile obtained.

To report at source level, i.e., to associate a "trace-DNA" profile with a body fluid such as blood, requires further information and separate presumptive, or RNA tests (heeding warnings already provided in Section 2.6 that associations of "trace-DNA" and body fluid are not implicit).

5.11.1 Evaluation of "Trace-DNA" Evidence That Has Not Followed from a DNA Database Search

The prosecution alleged that the knife was the murder weapon and the "trace-DNA" profiles obtained from the blade and the handle of the knife were put forward as evidence.

Ownership of the knife (found in a cutlery drawer of the suspect) was not disputed. Neither was it disputed that the victim and suspect had social contact (but the victim had never visited the premises of Sollecito). Given that the victim was allegedly stabbed by the suspect the primary consideration was whether there was *blood* from Kercher on the knife blade. The presence of DNA from Kercher was *secondary* to this question—if the DNA came from her skin cells or saliva, then the mere presence of matching DNA was not relevant to the crime event since the DNA could have been deposited before or afterward (Section 2.5).

Therefore, the presence of the DNA profiles, without any additional information, does not assist to support the prosecution's case to understand the *activity* of the stabbing event itself, to the exclusion of all other possible modes of transfer of the DNA evidence.

5.12 MODES OF TRANSFER: LIMITATIONS OF THE INFORMATION THAT CAN BE USED TO ASSESS THE RELEVANCE OF DNA PROFILING EVIDENCE

The responsibility of the forensic scientist is to put forward the "limitations" of the evidence so that it is not misinterpreted. The statement restricted to the *sub-source* level in the propositions framework is of limited use to the prosecution since a conviction must be "beyond reasonable doubt" and therefore it must include a statement of the "activity" that led to the DNA transfer.

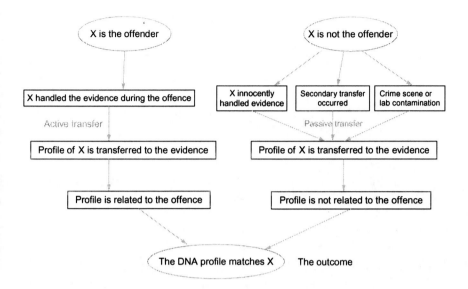

Figure 5.2 A flow diagram showing the various possible methods of DNA transfer. Note that the outcome of the DNA profile is the same regardless of the route that it took.

In a court examination of the forensic scientist, the prosecution lawyer will always question whether the evidence can be used to support a level higher than sub-source, and the forensic scientist must be very cautious when led down this inevitable line of questioning. The starting position is to explain all of the possible transfer methods described in Section 1.3 and illustrated in Figure 5.2.

5.12.1 Summary Starting Position

1. The forensic scientist only observes the "trace-DNA" profile. This profile by itself cannot be used to infer a cellular origin.
2. If there is more than one DNA profile in a mixture then they cannot be assumed to be deposited concurrently, neither can they be assumed to all follow the same transfer route. Each of the contributors to a DNA profile may follow the same or different routes.

5.12.2 Temporal Considerations

Transfer of DNA/body fluid may occur via one or more of the following routes:

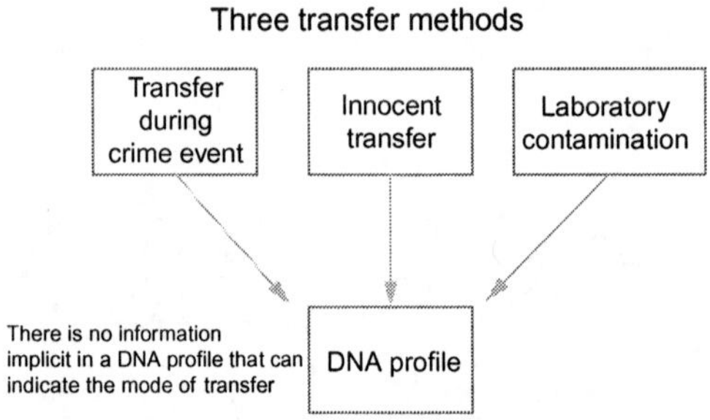

Three transfer methods

Figure 5.3 Mode of transfer. There are essentially three ways by which a DNA profile may become "evidential." Only one of these routes is associated with the crime event itself.

- The "trace-DNA"/body fluid was transferred before the crime event (innocent contact, background contamination)
- The "trace-DNA"/body fluid was transferred during the crime event
- The "trace-DNA"/body fluid was transferred after the crime event (investigator-mediated contamination)

Specific considerations (still at sub-source level) relating to the three possible modes of transfer of DNA evidence to the knife (item 36) are as follows (Figure 5.3):

1. Transfer during the crime event (Hp)?
   a. A "trace-DNA" profile matching Knox was found on the knife handle
   b. A "trace-DNA" profile matching Kercher was found on the knife blade
2. Innocent transfer (Hd)?
   a. The knife was found in a cutlery drawer in Sollecito's flat (previous innocent contact implied)
   b. The knife was described as "clean" and there was no evidence of blood
   c. The defendant and victim knew each other hence there was a chance that transfer could take place prior to the crime event by a method outlined in Figure 5.2
3. Laboratory contamination (Hd)?
   a. There were questions about how the material had been collected.
   b. Was there opportunity for DNA transfer during the collection process?
   c. Was there opportunity for DNA transfer within the packaging, or were items stored together?

Unfortunately, many of these questions are imponderable in the absence of relevant data that can be used. When trace amounts of DNA are evaluated, it becomes critical to understand the various possibilities of transfer outlined in Figure 5.2.

5.13 HOW WAS THE EVIDENCE INTERPRETED BY THE JUDGES?

5.13.1 Bathroom

Mixed traces of DNA attributed to Knox and Kercher were discovered in the shared bathroom. Blood was detected but there was no evidence that Knox was wounded. However, the Massei judgment (original conviction) contended that the mixtures were concurrent. There was little consideration about the expectations of the pre-existing background levels of DNA that would be present. Knox and Kercher shared the premises—their DNA will be everywhere. If blood is detected, it is clear that this does not automatically follow that *all* the DNA detected came from blood (Section 5.12).

However, the Massei judgment stated:

Amanda, soiled with Meredith's blood, entered the bathroom which was right next door to the room in which Meredith had been stabbed; putting her hand against the door she left a mark on it and the dribble of blood which remained is a sign [proof] of this, and left a mark also—still with Meredith's blood—on the light switch; she touched the cotton-bud box which was on the sink and left a mixed trace specimen of herself and of Meredith

Mixtures of Knox and Kercher were found in the washbasin and bidet and Massei inferred . . .

an activity that, through the action of rubbing, involved the cleaning of the victim's blood, and could involve the loss of the cells through exfoliation of whoever was cleaning themselves: the two biological traces thus united together in that single trace

To reiterate, these are statements that relate to the activity of transfer—not backed-up by scientific evidence beyond the sub-source inference. The expectation is that mixtures of DNA will be observed as natural background where people share premises. This expectation of mixtures also extends to visitors to premises. Therefore the limitations of interpretation of the DNA evidence are still firmly rooted at sub-source level.

5.13.2 The Bra-Clasp

Alternative "activity" propositions put forward by prosecution and defense were as follows:

1. Transfer during the crime event (Hp)
   a. Evidence: A DNA profiling matching Sollecito was found on the clasp

2. Innocent transfer (Hd)
   a. The defendant and victim knew each other hence there was a chance that transfer could take place prior to the crime event by a method outlined in Figure 5.2
3. Laboratory contamination (Hd)
   a. There were questions about how the material had been collected.
   b. Was there opportunity for DNA transfer during the collection process?
   c. Was there opportunity for DNA transfer within the packaging, or were items stored together?

The defense position is that Sollecito attempted to break down the door of Kercher's locked bedroom, when he realized that something was amiss. There was a 47 days interval between the discovery of the bra-clasp at the crime scene and its collection. During that time the clasp had been moved and was found under a rug. In addition, there is video footage of the clasp being passed round police scientists, dropped on the floor—and the suggestion that gloves used to handle the evidence were not changed in between handling different objects. Shoe covers were not changed as investigating officers walked through the crime scene.

The defense position is that there was an opportunity for DNA to be accidently transferred by investigators as they moved from room to room, touching door handles, and different items without changing gloves.

Y chromosome testing suggested the presence of three or more males, and the DNA mixture was from three or more people.

Alternatively, could any of the unknown males be a perpetrator?

5.13.3 Gloves

In a recent article by Szkuta et al. (2013), the authors compared the possibility of DNA transfer using items that are commonly used at crime scenes—namely scissors, gloves, and forceps in order to examine exhibits (Figure 5.4). A series of cotton swatches were prepared with small quantities (25 µl) of blood from a known individual. The stains were allowed to dry. Then they were handled with forceps, scissors, or latex gloves (in relation to the Kercher case we are primarily interested in the latter). Medium pressure was applied via a gloved thumb and index fingers with contact for 2–3 s. Then a secondary DNA-free substrate was touched. It was demonstrated that DNA profiles can be transferred from primary to secondary substrates. There

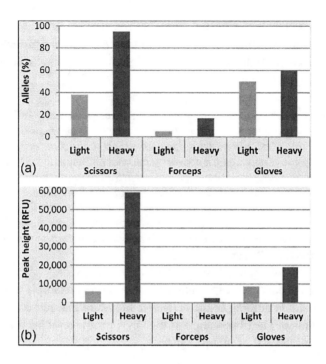

Figure 5.4 Average percentage of alleles transferred by each vector in both light and heavy contamination/contact scenarios (a) and the corresponding total peak heights of alleles transferred (b). (Source: From Figure 1 of Szkuta et al. (2013)).

is strong evidence to show that the failure of investigators to change their gloves in between handling items and potentially touching door handles is high risk, giving credibility to the defense proposition that Sollecito's DNA was transferred as a result of cross contamination.

More work is required in this area, however, and the experiments could be repeated to better reflect the conditions of the Kercher case, but the principle of cross transfer mediated by latex gloves is demonstrably high risk.

These concerns were not addressed in the Massei report.

5.13.4 The Judgment in Relation to the Knife (Exhibit 36)

The Massei report concluded:

… appears more likely to have been derived from her having held the knife to strike, rather than from having used it to cut some food.

Again the evidence was elevated from "sub-source" to proof of the "activity" of stabbing—even going so far as to mention that the presence of the DNA profile could be used to infer the angle at which the knife was held. The judgment continued:

> Remembering that this trace was found at the point in which the knife handle has a kind of upturn or rise [rialzo], after which the blade begins, with the knife positioned thus in a horizontal position with respect to the plane on which one is cutting [piano di appoggio], it appears somewhat unlikely to hypothesize that such a biological trace would have come to rest at the point indicated. Conversely, should the cutting implement be used for striking, and therefore moving it not horizontally, but with a certain inclination, it is quite probable for the hand holding the knife to undergo a sliding motion due to the violence required for the blow and, finishing up with a certain violence against said upturn, thereby leaving behind the biological trace.

However, this is dangerous speculation that is another example of confirmation bias—there is nothing in the scientific literature that remotely supports such an inference. The observation of the DNA profile remains firmly rooted at the sub-source level of interpretation.

5.13.5 The Burden of Proof and the Importance of Experimentation

A very important issue is raised in the Hellmann report (the judge who acquitted the defendants) that literally goes to the heart of the matter. The question raised was the "burden of proof." The conclusion of the Hellmann report in relation to the bra-clasp was as follows:

> In any case, the arguments set forth above, which refute the idea that the burden to prove the source of contamination rests on the defendant making that claim, should be recalled here: it is, on the contrary, those using that result [as evidence] to support an accusation who have to prove that the procedure and, prior to that, the collection stage happened in accordance with the methods and precautions necessary to avoid contamination. As noted above, this did not happen here.
> Therefore, the possibility of using the presence of Raffaele Sollecito's genetic profile on the hook of the bra as a reliable piece of circumstantial evidence ceases to exist.

The burden of proof is on the prosecution to prove beyond reasonable doubt that a series of events did occur and a series of events (i.e., innocent transfer) did not occur. Proving a negative is impossible—the unavoidable conclusion is: with cases of this kind, that no attempt should be made to interpret the evidence above the sub-source level proposition.

The way forward is to carry out proactive experimentation in order to understand the various modes of transfer, defined probabilistically, as demonstrated by the fingernails example in Chapter 3. Rather than to speculate, the court discussion must be rooted in science—i.e., to refer to peer-reviewed publications and data to support evaluations of evidence. To summarize:

- The scientist assists the court with a statement of limitations of the evidence (i.e., restricting interpretation to an appropriate level in the hierarchy.)
- If any of the possibilities are ranked then this is carried out relative to the peer-reviewed literature and experimentation.
- Were laboratory-environmental contamination records available for inspection? How were items packaged and transported? Were they examined in different facilities?
- The court has to decide whether the possibility that is put forward by the prosecution is robust so that all other possibilities are highly improbable, remembering that the burden of proof placed upon the prosecution must be "beyond reasonable doubt." The input of the scientist is key to the debate. Views must be firmly based in objective science following the framework in Chapter 3, rather than subjective speculation.

5.13.6 What Further Information Is Needed to Improve Understanding of DNA Distribution and Transfer at Crime Scenes

More basic research is needed to understand typical background DNA distributions:

1. What is the distribution of DNA profiles in premises where people cohabit?
2. What is the probability that visitors to premises will leave traces?
3. How long will the traces last for?
4. How does DNA transfer within a premises?
5. For example, if a door handle is "contaminated" with DNA from an individual, what is the chance that another individual will transfer this DNA to an item?
6. How does the physical presence of the investigator affect the background DNA?

7. If the investigator wears latex gloves that are not changed in between handling items in the premises, going from room to room, turning door handles, what is the chance that this will result in transfer of "evidential" DNA profiles?

Targeted research is required to understand if proposals put forward by the prosecution have support.

The judges in the Massei report concluded that the transfer of DNA from Amanda Knox to the handle of the knife was more likely to be a result of "stabbing the victim" rather than "preparation of food." If the knife had been used in the murder itself, it is undisputed that copious amounts of blood would be present upon the blade. Blood was not detected, however. The prosecution argument was that the knife had been cleaned and this was linked to a strong smell of bleach, the implication being that the knife had been cleaned with bleach. The question is whether bleach can alter the characteristics of the body fluid sufficiently so that DNA is positively tested and the test for blood is negative (since this is what the prosecution allege). Note that the work of Peel and Gill (2004) suggested that the body fluid test for blood was sensitive than the DNA test. But we could speculate endlessly...

5.14 A TARGETED PROTOCOL TO ASSESS THE PROSECUTION PROPOSITIONS

Forensic science should not be based upon "armchair arguments" about possibilities and theories discussed above. There is no substitute for experimentation.

To ascertain if the prosecution argument is credible, here is an experimental design:

1. Take a series of identical knife blades that have been pretreated to be DNA free
2. Cover with blood from a known individual
3. Allow to dry
4. Remove with bleach (the prosecution suggested that bleach was used to destroy evidence)—other methods of cleaning can be compared
5. Attempt to recover DNA from the knife blade
6. Carry out presumptive tests (and RNA-based tests) to determine the presence of blood
7. Compare results with a series of controls that have not been covered with blood

5.14.1 Is the Distribution of the DNA Profile on the Knife-Handle (Item 36) Consistent with the Activity of Stabbing?

In the Massei report it was held that the distribution of the DNA profiles on the knife was more likely to occur as a result of "stabbing." To discover whether there is any credibility with this suggestion, experiments are required. Here is another suggestion for an experimental design:

take a series of knives that are treated to be DNA free (remember to confirm this by taking control swabs):

Part I:

1. Subjects to use the knives in order to cut food
2. The same subjects to use different knives in order to stab dummies
3. The knife handles then analyzed for DNA profiles, and the distributions of DNA profiles assessed

Part II:

1. A series of identical knives can be used in the experiment. A set used to prepare food and a comparable set used to "stab dummies." The experiment requires that the distribution of the assailant's DNA is assessed

Part III:

The results from Part I and Part II are collated and experts asked to distinguish between knives used to cut food vs. those used in stabbing based on the distribution of the DNA profiles of the handler.

5.14.2 Background Contamination and the Bra-Clasp

Another experimental design is needed to examine the issue of the background contamination and the bra-clasp. Of course these experiments will need to take place at a "simulated crime scene."

We specifically ask: What are the expectation of levels of background DNA expected on the bra-clasp given that it was not recovered for more than 40 days and it was moved within the crime scene?

To investigate, take a series of cotton swatches. Deposit them in a room. Leave for several weeks. Simulate the investigation by handling with latex gloves. These cotton swatches act as control samples and either they will be "contaminated" or they will be "clean."

In this case, there are specific circumstances that are proposed by both the prosecution and the defense. The problem is that the court debate has been based on speculation rather than experimentation—the latter is needed for any scientific debate—see Chapter 3.

5.15 FINAL REMARKS

Whereas it is easy to design experiments in order to test hypotheses above, it is more difficult to "back-track" to discover incidents of contamination that have arisen directly as a result of transferring evidential items to laboratories. Once a crime scene is compromised, for example, by failure to change latex gloves, nothing can be done to restore the integrity of the crime scene to its original position.

The default position is that DNA fragments are highly mobile within the environment (demonstrated within the *laboratory*; Vandewoestyne et al., 2011; Witt et al., 2009). In relation to packaged items, Goray et al. (2012a) in a publication entitled *"DNA transfer within forensic exhibit packaging: Potential for DNA loss and relocation"* concluded:

> Significant quantities of DNA are frequently: a) transferred from the exhibit and/or to other exhibits within the same package; b) transferred from its area of initial deposit to other areas of the same exhibit and/or to other exhibits within the same package.

It was highlighted that significant attention to detail was required when exhibits were transported to the laboratory. Other possible cross contamination routes include examination of items in close proximity to each other (e.g., Adam Scott, Jama). One of the experiments carried out by Goray included a study on the effect of transportation of knives in cardboard tubes. Apart from DNA loss by transfer to the container walls, it was shown that the DNA was redistributed so that profiles on the blade ended up on the handle and vice versa. Recall that the knife item 36 was repackaged in a shoe box that was not DNA free (and it is unknown what it previously contained). There was opportunity for DNA to transfer from the walls of the shoe box to the knife, and vice versa. This important finding by Goray et al. is also highly significant with respect to the conclusion of the Massei report claiming that the distribution of DNA on the knife supported the hypothesis of stabbing motion.

In a wider context, as DNA profiling methods have become more sensitive, there is naturally a desire to reopen unsolved cases in the hope that DNA evidence can be used to "solve crimes." Many of these cases predate DNA profiling when it was commonplace for items to be examined together and to be kept together in large paper bags. However, Goray also shows that these conditions are ideal to allow transfer of DNA within and between packages. Therefore, this places serious constraints on interpretation where there are distinct possibilities that such transfers can have occurred.

Items in a case progress from the crime scene to a recovery unit where the items are examined on a bench and then sent to a DNA unit where the profiling is carried out and the reports prepared. At each stage, there is a possibility of cross contamination from other items, from the investigators themselves, or from poor packaging. However, the levels of cross contamination can only be ascertained by proactive assessment.

In many labs, significant efforts are carried out to discover if an investigator has cross contaminated an item with his own DNA (by comparison with a database of investigator DNA profiles). Conversely there is little proactive effort to determine the extent of cross contamination between items that are submitted to laboratories and this is clearly a weakness.

Given that errors are possible at every level of the investigation, a blind trial system needs to be devised around mock cases that are carefully prepared, as far as possible without the individuals' knowledge. These mock cases would be processed the same as real casework, and the resulting reports would be scrutinized by a quality assurance unit. This would at least provide a level of confidence in a laboratory process. Until such exercises become routine in jurisdictions then the issues of contamination (which seems to be a key consideration in the Murder of Meredith Kercher and other cases discussed in this book) will remain imponderable.

The most important advice is to "recognize the limitations" that can be adduced from evidence, otherwise the scientist, and everyone else in the criminal justice system is led down the path of "confirmation bias" where the evidence is subconsciously "fitted" to the prosecution explanation of the evidence. Always provide *all* of the alternative explanations and never express a personal preference on source or activity level propositions, unless it is backed up by solid peer-reviewed research; anything else is mere "speculation" that courts may well confuse with "expert opinion." Never transpose a likelihood ratio from the sub-source to the source level. A true expert does not rely upon personal opinion to express a view. He or she argues a position only from the perspective of the scientific literature. If the relevant experiments have not been carried out to answer a case-related point, then the position is unknown. I finish with a quote from the excellent report (Vincent, 2010) of R. v. Jama (Section 2.2.3):

> *Precisely how it may have happened cannot be determined as the deposition of the minute amount of material involved could have occurred in a number of ways. It is possible to speculate about the probability of transference through various mechanisms, but ultimately it is pointless to do so.*

Recommendation 1: The expert should provide the court with an unbiased list of all possible modes of transfer of DNA evidence (Section 1.7).

Recommendation 2:

• If a negative control shows a partial, or full, DNA profile, then this indicates that the batch of samples concurrently processed may be compromised and should be completely rerun.
• There may be implications for the casework procedure in general and the source of the profile should be investigated by comparison with staff elimination databases, the national DNA database (NDNAD), and any other samples processed during a relevant period of time (see Section 2.1).

Recommendation 3: The possibility of investigator-mediated contamination outside the laboratory environment cannot be excluded. The laboratory cannot dismiss the possibility by proxy of its own protocols and practice (Section 2.2).

Recommendation 4: If a body fluid is identified from a known contributor this information cannot be used to hypothesize the body fluid origin of any additional contributor in a mixture of body fluids/tissues (Section 2.6).

Recommendation 5: To formulate sets of alternative hypotheses, they must be logically constructed, so that the alternatives mirror each other. Different hypotheses must never be combined together (unless supported by formal probabilistic analysis) (Section 2.7.1).

Recommendation 6: Assessments of the probative value of DNA evidence from any crime stain where two or more individuals are in admixture requires formal probabilistic analysis, rather than counting the number of alleles that match a suspect. The counting method can be very misleading (Section 2.7).

Recommendation 7: If analyses are replicated and/or several stains are analyzed, this is an excellent way to reduce the impact of contamination rates. In Scott only one stain out of five tested showed his DNA profile and this is characteristic of contamination. In Jama, the result was not replicated since only one swab in four showed a DNA profile, but this advice will not apply if the item itself is grossly contaminated (Section 2.12.1).

Recommendation 8: The strength of evidence of a "trace-DNA" profile is always assessed at the sub-source level and this cannot be transposed to the source-level to imply that the DNA is from a particular body fluid (the uncertainty of the association will require a different statistic to be calculated) (Section 2.12.2).

Recommendation 9: If a scientist expresses an opinion, then this opinion must be qualified by experimental evidence. If an opinion is expressed that appears to have no supporting evidence (in terms of peer review or data analysis) so that it cannot be tested objectively, then it has no scientific basis (Section 3.6.1.2).

Recommendation 10: To mitigate the effect of the "confirmation bias," the assessment of the non-DNA evidence should be carried out independently of the DNA evidence (Section 4.8).

Recommendations 11:

1. Much more emphasis to be placed upon error rate discovery—that is, proactive involvement of regulatory authorities is needed—blind trials need to be propagated.
2. In the absence of an error rate, a proxy (nonzero) error rate(s) needs serious consideration (Section 4.27).

Recommendation 12:

1. Investigators to be trained to carry out "strength of evidence calculations" that combine DNA with non-DNA evidence using a Bayesian framework. A simple demonstration is provided in Section 4.25 where the basic formula is provided.
2. The "other (non-DNA) evidence" in a case should be evaluated. What numeric level of "other evidence" is required in order for the totality of evidence to be probative?

3. Use of geographic profiling is useful to inform the size of the target population and to refine the weights applied to Bayesian calculations (Section 4.18).

4. Training is required to ensure that investigators are aware of cognitive biases and are able to recognize the effects

Recommendation 13: To assess the background levels of DNA present in the laboratory, environmental monitoring is required. Continuity of case items should include documentation to show that they have been properly packaged, stored, transported and examined in an environment that is designed to minimize the possibility of cross transfer between them. Sensitive items will need to be examined in separate facilities to preclude the possibility of cross contamination (Section 5.2).

Active Transfer

Active transfer is associated with direct (touching) transfer of DNA during the crime-event itself—e.g., by sexual assault and transfer of sperm to the victim; a victim scratches an assailant and a DNA profile is transferred underneath fingernails (Chapter 3) (Section 1.3).

Complex DNA profile

A DNA profile that comprises DNA from more than one individual in admixture. If the DNA is low level then alleles may be absent, resulting in missing allelic components (drop-out). In addition, a contamination effect known as drop-in, may result in one or two additional alleles that are not from any of the main contributors to the profile (Section 4.2).

Confirmation bias

Confirmation bias begins with the scientist/investigator "searching for evidence" to discover a perpetrator of some offence. "Locard's exchange principle"[1]: "every contact leaves a trace" drives the "expectation" that the discovery of a DNA profile must be significant in relation to crime. This may give the investigator an illusion of objectivity where none exists. This is called "confirmation bias." If a DNA profile is discovered, and a match with a man is obtained, he becomes a suspect, and then the machinery of justice places him center stage. The interpretation of the evidence is anchored on the suspect. The DNA profile may match the suspect—but how confident can we be that the DNA profile that has been recovered is *relevant* to the crime event itself (Section 1.3.9)?

Contamination

1. Background contamination: People who inhabit premises, along with their visitors, will both shed their DNA so that it will be all pervasive in the environment. It will be present on surfaces as "sticky DNA" and in aerosol as "house dust" or saliva spray. Background contaminating DNA

---

[1] Dr. Edmond Locard (December 13, 1877-May 4, 1966) was a French pioneer in forensic science.

remains intact for months, if not years after deposition, provided that the environment is dry.

2. Investigator-mediated contamination: This kind of contamination is outside the "natural environment" of the case. It is mediated by investigators who unwittingly contaminate the crime scene with their own DNA. Disposable paper suits and gloves worn by investigators may inadvertently transfer "sticky DNA" from one part of the crime scene to another (e.g., by not changing gloves in between examination of items). Once items are packaged and transported for analysis, e.g., a knife or some clothing, "aerosol DNA" can redistribute itself both within and between poorly packaged evidential items (Goray et al., 2012a). Laboratory contamination includes contamination of plasticware and reagents, either at the manufacturing source or within the laboratory itself (Gill et al., 2010; Tamariz et al., 2006) (Section 1.3).

CSI effect

A belief that real forensic science is based on TV shows that glamorize crime-scene investigation. A contributing factor to confirmation bias and false deductive logic.

Framework of propositions

The role of the forensic scientist is to provide an objective assessment of the evidence. Interpretation of evidence within a "framework of propositions." The framework provides an hierarchy where the probative value of the evidence increases with each level and is described as follows:

1. The *subsource* level refers to the strength of evidence of the DNA profile itself.
2. The *source* level refers to an evaluation of strength of evidence if a DNA profile can be associated with a particular body fluid, such as semen, or blood.
3. The *activity* level associates the DNA profile with the crime itself, e.g., sexual assault.
4. The highest level deals with the *ultimate issue* of guilt/innocence. (Section 1.7).

Likelihood ratio

A preferred method to report evidence (although it is not universal). The ratio of two probabilities of the same event evaluated under two different hypotheses or propositions. For DNA profiling it is usually expressed as the probability of the evidence if the DNA profile came from the suspect (the numerator) compared to the probability of the evidence if it came from an unknown, unrelated person (the denominator). Likelihood ratios are very flexible; multiple contributors or relatives of the suspect can be evaluated. Often a known person (the victim) will be conditioned in the denominator (Section 1.6).

Matching allele count

An attempt is made to associate a crime-stain by counting the number of alleles that happen to match a suspect. Some verbal strength of evidence is used to associate the crime stain with the DNA profile of a suspect. The method is strongly discouraged as it is nonscientific for reasons explained in Section 4.28, and is prone to confirmation bias.

National DNA database

There are two kinds of DNA databases: (a) A collection of reference profiles from suspects, usually collected by buccal scrapes and (b) a smaller collection of crime-stains is held in a separate database. Matches are obtained by comparing (a) with (b) and a strength of evidence in the form of a likelihood ratio or match probability is given in a written statement (Section 4.2).

Passive transfer

Passive transfer results in the "background" distribution of DNA profiles that pre-exists the crime scene. The population of DNA profiles is derived by any of the mechanisms described below:

- Direct transfer: touching
- Aerosol transfer: speaking, exhaling (saliva spray); skin cells (as housedust); transfer within and between poorly packaged items
- Indirect transfer: secondary transfer—an intermediary transfers a DNA profile on a surface, object or person to another surface, object, or person (Section 1.3).

Scientific method

Defined by the Oxford English Dictionary as: *a method or procedure that has characterized natural science since the 17th century, consisting in systematic observation, measurement, and experiment, and the formulation, testing, and modification of hypotheses* (Section 4.31).

Statement of limitations

The "statement of limitations" is the starting position to interpret "trace-DNA" evidence.

1. Although a DNA profile has been obtained, it is not possible to identify the type of cells from which the DNA originated, neither is it possible to state *when* the cells were deposited.
2. It is not possible to make any conclusion about *transfer and persistence* of DNA in this case. It is not possible to estimate when the suspect last wore the [watch],[2] if it is his DNA.
3. Because the DNA test is very sensitive, it is not unexpected to find mixtures. If the potential origins of DNA profiles cannot be identified, it does not necessarily follow that they are relevant to this case, since transfer of cells can occur as a result of casual contact (Section 1.2.1).

Sticky-DNA

A term to convey the idea that secondary transfer is mediated by the sticky nature of DNA on surfaces (Section 1.3).

The association fallacy

A probability is transposed from one level of the framework of propositions to higher level. For example, the strength of evidence of a subsource DNA profile may be directly applied to a source, e.g., blood. The fallacy is to assume that the likelihood ratio of the subsource level is the same as the source level. The uncertainty of the association of the DNA profile with its source will reduce the combined strength of evidence (Section 1.5.1).

The compounded error effect

Several errors are propagated within a specific case (one error leads to another). For example, the association fallacy leads to wrongful association of a DNA profile with a body fluid, such as semen. The presence of semen indicates sexual activity, which in turn is very close to the ultimate issue of guilt/innocence (Section 1.5.4).

The defendant's double fallacy

Defendant's fallacy is not a fallacy under some circumstances listed below. If a defendant is discovered by a database trawl, where there is no other evidence in the case, then the evidence should be interpreted using

---

[2]This statement was originally used in relation to DNA evidence found on a watch found at a crime scene.

a Bayesian model, incorporating the Target population. This will assist to place the DNA evidence into perspective.

- The background population has been filtered so that the target population comprises individuals of the correct age group, geographical location, reduced by the database search, etc., so that each individual is equally likely to be the culprit, before the DNA evidence is assessed.
- Note that if the other evidence is exculpatory for an individual identified by database search, then the odds of guilt are reduced further.

Commentators on the defendant's fallacy have readily assumed that courts never convict unless the non-DNA evidence is probative. However, the cases discussed in this book suggest that this premise is incorrect. Unfortunately in most of the appeals discussed, the other evidence is usually limited, and may be exculpatory. The court may over rely upon the "swamping effect" (Section 4.17) of the DNA evidence to absorb non-DNA neutral or exculpatory evidence. In the absence of the correct calculations the effect will tend to reinforce "confirmation bias" (Section 4.22).

The defendant's fallacy
The "defendant's fallacy" or the "defence lawyer fallacy" is frequently quoted as an error of logic. The fallacy would argue that since the expected number of people in the target population is 800,000 and the profile frequency is 1/40,000; given the probability that the defendant is the culprit is 0.047 (from the equation above) we expect there to be approximately $1/0.047 \approx 20$(unknown) people with the same profile characteristics. The fallacy is committed if not all individuals are equally likely to have committed the offence, before the knowledge of the DNA evidence.

The false negative error
For example, a DNA profile is obtained but its source is not identified (this error is harmless in the sense that the strength of evidence is reported at sub-source level) (Section 4.2.1).

The false positive error
For example, a body fluid or cellular source is identified from a questioned crime sample, but in truth the DNA profile is from a different body fluid/cellular source. Either the body fluid is from a donor who is not the suspect or the presumptive test has reacted to something other than the targeted body fluid (Section 4.24).

The hidden perpetrator effect

A crime stain is recovered. The expectation is that DNA has been transferred during the course of an offence (such as sexual assault). In reality no such transfer of DNA is detected, although body fluid transfer cannot be eliminated. It is likely that DNA from innocent individuals will be implicated as potential offenders and the true perpetrator effectively eliminated from the enquiry.

Note the converse will also apply. A perpetrator may have been correctly identified, but his DNA may be absent from the crime scene. DNA from innocent people may be recovered from the crime scene instead. The perpetrator may argue that his absence of a DNA profile, and the presence of other unexplained DNA profiles proves his innocence. This sequence of events is quite common in "cold-case reviews" where old cases are reopened for investigation. Here the miscarriage of justice results in a correctly identified perpetrator being released because of the illogical reasoning explained above (Section 1.5.2).

The mind projection fallacy

Characterized by Jaynes 1991 as: someone's subjective judgments are "projected" onto the real world, rather than being related to personal perception. If the fallacy is committed by the scientist it leads to the "compounded error" effect. A subjective (personal) opinion may be expressed as "expert opinion" and confused with "scientific evidence" (where in fact none exists). Courts are particularly vulnerable to this effect since the resources required to challenge expert opinion are often limited (Section 2.12.2.1).

The naïve investigator effect

The naïve investigator effect is inspired by the case of wrongful arrest of Adam Scott[TM] where a man was arrested, accused of rape and incarcerated on the basis of a DNA profile match resulting from a contamination incident (Section 2.1). The DNA profile was eventually traced to a contamination incident, but the case is notable because the match was adventitiously obtained from a search of the national DNA database. The exculpatory evidence was initially ignored. To summarize the definition: the naïve investigator finds the closest match to a crime stain in a national DNA database, he ignores exculpatory evidence and seeks to prosecute the matching individual, ignoring other evidence in the case. The effect is also apparent in the other miscarriages of justice, that do not require a national DNA database to identify a suspect: notably in the "Death of Meredith Kercher" where the investigator retrieves DNA profiles from a premises;

assumes it to be from a perpetrator. Confirmation bias takes over and the "association fallacy" is used to construct an illogical chain of events that are prosecution biased (Section 1.5.3).

The prosecutor's fallacy

A common mistake is to "transpose the conditional" (the Prosecutor's fallacy); the mistake is to evaluate $Pr(Hp|E)$ and $Pr(Hd|E)$ instead of $Pr(E|Hp)$ and $Pr(E|Hd)$. The prosecutor's fallacy is committed as a verbal error. For example the scientist may say: "The probability *that* the DNA profile came from someone other than Mr. S is one in one billion." The key to understanding the fallacy is the choice of words—the use of the word *if* in the first statement makes the connection between E and H in $Pr(E|H)$ clear, whereas as the word *that* implies $(PrH|E)$. For a full discussion see Evett and Weir (1998, pp. 227–231) (Section 1.6).

The random man adventitious match

A match between a questioned DNA profile from a crime stain and a suspect who is not its donor. The chance of a questioned sample matching one or more reference samples on a database size N with a match probability p is $1 - (1 - p)^N$. The genotypes are identical by chance. A way to distinguish between them will be to increase the number of loci used in the test (Section 2.4.2).

The same man adventitious match

Suspect A has been apprehended and placed on the National DNA database. His reference DNA profile matches DNA extracted from Case A or Item A. A contamination event occurs so that DNA is transferred between case A or item A to an unrelated case B or item B. Then the DNA profile of case B/item B will match the reference profile of suspect A. The genotypes of the profiles from questioned stains A and B are identical as they originate from the same individual (Section 2.4.2).

The serial error effect

The same kinds of errors are propagated across unrelated offences. An example is the use of a presumptive test for explosives being reported as "definitive" in the series of 1970s terrorist cases reported in the United Kingdom. Phantom of Heilbronn is an example (Section 2.3.1).

The swamping effect

A court is provided with an enormous DNA match probability of one in one billion (for example) and this overrides any other information that may suggest that the defendant is innocent. Typically a court is not provided with an indication of the error rate, or will not be provided with the information that the suspect was discovered by database trawl. These factors have an important bearing on the interpretation of evidence yet the court will be provided with no guidance how to interpret the numeric DNA evidence in the context of the nonnumeric, other nonevidence, in a case. The strength of evidence cannot be assessed by intuitive methods alone, because innate cognitive biases will cause errors of judgment (Section 4.17).

The target population

The population identified to contain the perpetrator with some measurable probability based on geographic profiling evidence. The population may be filtered to restrict the target population to males of a given age group. Other relevant factors, such as ethnic group may be employed if there is sufficient evidence (Section 4.4).

Trace-DNA

"Trace-DNA" is defined as any sample where there is uncertainty that it may be associated with the crime event itself—so that it is possible that the transfer may have occurred *before* the crime event (innocent transfer) or *after* the crime event (investigator mediated) (Section 1.2).

The definition is deliberately vague: it hinges upon an assessment of the *relevance* of a "trace-DNA" profile to the crime event which is considered in the context of a "statement of limitations" (Section 1.2.1).

Transcription error

An error where an analyst makes a mistake to designate a DNA profile so that it is incorrectly recorded. If the sample is searched against the national DNA database it will fail to match a reference sample from a donor (if present) (Section 2.3.1).

BIBLIOGRAPHY

Aitken, C., Taroni, F., 2004. Statistics and the Evaluation of Evidence for Forensics Scientists. Wiley, Chichester.

Anon., 2009. Phantom of Heilbronn. Wikipedia.org, http://en.wikipedia.org/wiki/Phantom_of_Heilbronn

Anon., 2012a. CSI effect, Wikipedia.org, http://en.wikipedia.org/wiki/CSI_effect

Anon., 2012b. Death of Gareth Williams, Wikipedia.org, http://en.wikipedia.org/wiki/Death_of_Gareth_Williams

Balding, D.J., 2005. Weight-of-Evidence for Forensic DNA Profiles. Wiley, Chichester.

Balding, D.J., 2013. Evaluation of mixed-source, low-template DNA profiles in forensic science. Proc. Natl. Acad. Sci. U.S.A. 110, 12241–12246.

Balding, D.J., Buckleton, J., 2009. Interpreting low template DNA profiles. Forensic Sci. Int. Genet. 4, 1–10.

Balding, D.J., Donnelly, P., 1994. The prosecutor's fallacy and DNA evidence. Crim. Law Rev. 711–721. Bon article sur la Prosecutor's Fallacy.

Balding, D., Donnelly, P., 1996. Evaluating DNA profile evidence when the suspect is identified through a database search. J. Forensic Sci. 41, 603–607.

Ballantyne, K.N., Poy, A.L., van Oorschot, R.A., 2013. Environmental DNA monitoring: beware of the transition to more sensitive typing methodologies. Aust. J. Forensic Sci. 45, 323–340.

Biedermann, A., Taroni, F., 2012. Bayesian networks for evaluating forensic DNA profiling evidence: a review and guide to literature. Forensic Sci. Int. Genet. 6, 147–157.

Bleka, Ø., Dørum, G., Haned, H., Gill, P., 2014. Database extraction strategies for low-template evidence. Forensic Sci. Int. Genet. 9, 134–141.

Bright, J.-A., Taylor, D., Curran, J., Buckleton, J., 2014. Searching mixed DNA profiles directly against profile databases. Forensic Sci. Int. Genet. 9, 102–110.

Buckleton, J., Triggs, C., Walsh, S., 2004. Forensic DNA evidence interpretation. CRC, Boca Raton, FL.

Buckleton, J., Triggs, C., Champod, C., 2006. An extended likelihood ratio framework for interpreting evidence. Sci. Justice 46, 69–78.

Buckleton, J., Curran, J., Gill, P., 2007. Towards understanding the effect of uncertainty in the number of contributors to DNA stains. Forensic Sci. Int. Genet. 1, 20–28.

Butler, J.M., 2005. Forensic DNA Typing: Biology, Technology and Genetics Behind STR Markers. Elsevier Academic Press, Burlington, MA.

Butler, J.M., 2009. Fundamentals of Forensic DNA Typing. Academic Press, Burlington, MA.

Butler, J.M., 2011. Advanced Topics in Forensic DNA Typing: Methodology. Academic Press, San Diego, CA.

Cerri, N., Verzeletti, A., Cortellini, V., Cincotta, A., De Ferrari, F., 2009. Prevalence of mixed DNA profiles in fingernail swabs from autoptic cases. Forensic Sci. Int. Genet. Suppl. Ser. 2, 163–164.

Cook, O., Dixon, L., 2007. The prevalence of mixed DNA profiles in fingernail samples taken from individuals in the general population. Forensic Sci. Int. Genet. 1, 62–68.

Cook, R., Evett, I., Jackson, G., Jones, P., Lambert, J., 1998. A hierarchy of propositions: deciding which level to address in casework. Sci. Justice 38, 231–239.

ENFSI, 2008. Guidance on the production of best practice manuals within ENFSI, http://www.enfsi.eu/sites/default/files/documents/bylaws/guidance_document_for_best_practice_manuals.pdf

ENFSI 2014 Document on DNA-Database Management. http://www.enfsi.eu/sites/default/files/documents/enfsi_2014_document_on_dna-database_management_0.pdf

ENFSI survey on DNA databases in Europe December 2013 (published 2014). http://www.enfsi.eu/sites/default/files/documents/enfsi_survey_on_dna_databases_in_europe_december_2013_1.pdf

Evett, I., Weir, B., 1998. Interpreting DNA Evidence. Sinauer, Sunderland, MA.

Evett, I., Jackson, G., Lambert, J., 2000. More on the hierarchy of propositions: exploring the distinction between explanations and propositions. Sci. Justice 40, 3–10.

Evett, I., Gill, P., Jackson, G., Whitaker, J., Champod, C., 2002. Interpreting small quantities of DNA: the hierarchy of propositions and the use of Bayesian networks. J. Forensic Sci. 47, 520–530.

Finnebraaten, M., Granér, T., Hoff-Olsen, P., 2008. May a speaking individual contaminate the routine DNA laboratory? Forensic Sci. Int. Genet. Suppl. Ser. 1, 421–422.

Flanagan, N., McAlister, C., 2011. The transfer and persistence of DNA under the fingernails following digital penetration of the vagina. Forensic Sci. Int. Genet. 5, 479–483.

Fraser, J., Williams, R., 2009. Handbook of Forensic Science. Willan Publishing, Cullompton, Devon. ISBN: 978-1-84392-311-4.

Gill, P., 2001. Application of low copy number DNA profiling. Croat. Med. J. 42, 229–232.

Gill, P., 2002. Role of short tandem repeat DNA in forensic casework in the UK—past, present, and future perspectives. BioTechniques 32, 366–368, 370, 372, passim.

Gill, P., Buckleton, J., 2010. A universal strategy to interpret DNA profiles that does not require a definition of low-copy-number. Forensic Sci. Int. Genet. 4, 221–227.

Gill, P., Haned, H., 2013. A new methodological framework to interpret complex DNA profiles using likelihood ratios. Forensic Sci. Int. Genet. 7, 251–263.

Gill, P., Kirkham, A., 2004. Development of a simulation model to assess the impact of contamination in casework using STRs. J. Forensic Sci. 49, 485–491.

Gill, P., Werrett, D.J., 1987. Exclusion of a man charged with murder by DNA fingerprinting. Forensic Sci. Int. 35, 145–148.

Gill, P., Whitaker, J., Flaxman, C., Brown, N., Buckleton, J., 2000. An investigation of the rigor of interpretation rules for STRs derived from less than 100 pg of DNA. Forensic Sci. Int. 112, 17–40.

Gill, P., Fereday, L., Morling, N., Schneider, P.M., 2006a. New multiplexes for Europe-amendments and clarification of strategic development. Forensic Sci. Int. 163, 155–157.

Gill, P., Fereday, L., Morling, N., Schneider, P.M., 2006b. The evolution of DNA databases—recommendations for new European STR loci. Forensic Sci. Int. 156, 242–244.

Gill, P., Rowlands, D., Tully, G., Bastisch, I., Staples, T., Scott, P., 2010. Manufacturer contamination of disposable plastic-ware and other reagents—an agreed position statement by ENFSI, SWGDAM and BSAG. Forensic Sci. Int. Genet. 4, 269–270.

Gill, P., Gusmão, L., Haned, H., Mayr, W., Morling, N., Parson, W., et al., 2012. DNA Commission of the International Society of Forensic Genetics: recommendations on the evaluation of STR typing results that may include drop-out and/or drop-in using probabilistic methods. Forensic Sci. Int. Genet. 6, 679–688.

Gill, P., Bleka, Ø., Egeland, T., 2014. Comparison of the matching allele count method with the likelihood ratio method when complex DNA profiles are searched against a large National DNA database. Forensic Sci. Int. Genet. (in press).

Goray, M., Mitchell, R.J., van Oorschot, R.A., 2010a. Investigation of secondary DNA transfer of skin cells under controlled test conditions. Leg. Med. 12, 117–120.

Goray, M., Eken, E., Mitchell, R.J., van Oorschot, R.A., 2010b. Secondary DNA transfer of biological substances under varying test conditions. Forensic Sci. Int. Genet. 4, 62–67.

Goray, M., van Oorschot, R., Mitchell, J., 2012a. DNA transfer within forensic exhibit packaging: potential for DNA loss and relocation. Forensic Sci. Int. Genet. 6, 158–166.

Goray, M., Mitchell, J.R., van Oorschot, R.A., 2012b. Evaluation of multiple transfer of DNA using mock case scenarios. Leg. Med. 14, 40–46.

Guidance Booklet for Experts—Disclosure: Experts' Evidence, Case Management and Unused Material, 2010. http://www.cps.gov.uk/legal/assets/uploads/files/Guidance_for_Experts_-_2010_edition.pdf

Haned, H., 2011. Forensim: an open-source initiative for the evaluation of statistical methods in forensic genetics. Forensic Sci. Int. Genet. 5(4), 265–268.

Haned, H., Gill, P., 2011. Analysis of complex DNA mixtures using the Forensim package. Forensic Sci. Int. Genet. Suppl. Ser. 3, e79–e80.

Haned, H., Slooten, K., Gill, P., 2012. Exploratory data analysis for the interpretation of low template DNA mixtures. Forensic Sci. Int. Genet. 6, 762–774.

Harteveld, J., Lindenbergh, A., Sijen, T., 2013. RNA cell typing and DNA profiling of mixed samples: can cell types and donors be associated? Sci. Justice 53, 261–269.

Henderson, A., Lai, K., Power, T., Samson, O., Scott, S., Vintiner, S., 2004. Prevalence of foreign DNA under fingernails. In: Proceedings Challenges and Changes 17th International Symposium on the Forensic Sciences, Wellington.

Hicks, T., Taroni, F., Curran, J., Buckleton, J., Ribaux, O., Castella, V., 2010a. Use of DNA profiles for investigation using a simulated national DNA database. Part I. Partial SGM plus profiles. Forensic Sci. Int. Genet. 4, 232–238.

Hicks, T., Taroni, F., Curran, J., Buckleton, J., Castella, V., Ribaux, O., 2010b. Use of DNA profiles for investigation using a simulated national DNA database. Part II. Statistical and ethical considerations on familial searching. Forensic Sci. Int. Genet. 4, 316–322.

Hill, R., 2004. Multiple sudden infant deaths—coincidence or beyond coincidence? Paediatr. Perinat. Epidemiol. 18, 320–326.

Jaynes, E., 1991. Notes on present status and future prospects. In: Grandy, W.T., Schick, L.H. (Eds.), Maximum Entropy and Bayesian Methods. Kluwer Academic Press, Dordrecht, pp. 1–13.

Kent, J., Leitner, M., Curtis, A., 2006. Evaluating the usefulness of functional distance measures when calibrating journey-to-crime distance decay functions. Comput. Environ. Urban Syst. 30, 181–200.

Kirkham, A., Haley, J., Haile, Y., Grout, A., Kimpton, C., Al-Marzouqi, A., et al. 2013. High-throughput analysis using AmpFLSTR identifiler with the applied biosystems 3500xl genetic analyser. Forensic Sci. Int. Genet. 7, 92–97.

Koehler, J.J., 1996. The base rate fallacy reconsidered: descriptive, normative, and methodological challenges. Behav. Brain Sci. 19, 1–17.

Koehler, J., 2010. Proficiency tests to estimate error rates in the forensic sciences. Northwestern Public Law Research Paper No. 11–17, http://papers.ssrn.com/sol3/papers.cfm?abstract_id=1755665

Lindenbergh, A., Maaskant, P., Sijen, T., 2013. Implementation of RNA profiling in forensic casework. Forensic Sci. Int. Genet. 7(1), 159–166.

Lowe, A., Murray, C., Whitaker, J., Tully, G., Gill, P., 2002. The propensity of individuals to deposit DNA and secondary transfer of low level DNA from individuals to inert surfaces. Forensic Sci. Int. 129, 25–34.

Lynch, M., McNally, R., 2003. "Science," "common sense," and DNA evidence: a legal controversy about the public understanding of science. Public Underst. Sci. 12, 83–103.

Malsom, S., Flanagan, N., McAlister, C., Dixon, L., 2009. The prevalence of mixed DNA profiles in fingernail samples taken from couples who co-habit using autosomal and Y-STRs. Forensic Sci. Int. Genet. 3, 57–62.

Matte, M., Williams, L., Frappier, R., Newman, J., 2012. Prevalence and persistence of foreign DNA beneath fingernails. Forensic Sci. Int. Genet. 6, 236–243.

Meakin, G., Jamieson, A., 2013. DNA transfer: review and implications for casework. Forensic Sci. Int. Genet. 7, 434–443.

Meester, R., Sjerps, M., 2003. The evidential value in the DNA database search controversy and the two-stain problem. Biometrics 59, 727–732.

Meester, R., Sjerps, M., 2004. Why the effect of prior odds should accompany the likelihood ratio when reporting DNA evidence. Law Probab. Risk 3, 51–62.

National Research Council, 1992. DNA Technology in Forensic Science. The National Academy Press, Washington, DC.

National Research Council, 1996. The Evaluation of Forensic DNA Evidence: An Update. The National Academy Press, Washington, DC.

Paoletti, D., Doom, T., Krane, C., Raymer, M., Krane, D., 2005. Empirical analysis of the STR profiles resulting from conceptual mixtures. J. Forensic Sci. 50, 1361.

Peel, C., Gill, P., 2004. Attribution of DNA profiles to body fluid stains. In: Doutremépuich, Ch., Morling, N. (Eds.), 20th Congress of the International Society for Forensic Genetics Arcachon, France, 2003 International Congress Series, vol. 1261. Elsevier, Amsterdam Lausanne New York Oxford., pp. 53–55.

Perlin, M.W., Sinelnikov, A., 2009. An information gap in DNA evidence interpretation. PLoS One 4, e8327.

Pope, S., Clayton, T., Whitaker, J., Lowe, J., Puch-Solis, R., 2009. More for the same? Enhancing the investigative potential of forensic DNA databases. Forensic Sci. Int. Genet. Suppl. Ser. 2, 458–459.

Port, N.J., Bowyer, V.L., Graham, E.A., Batuwangala, M.S., Rutty, G.N., 2006. How long does it take a static speaking individual to contaminate the immediate environment? Forensic Sci. Med. Pathol. 2, 157–163.

Poy, A.L., van Oorschot, R.A., 2006. Trace DNA presence, origin, and transfer within a forensic biology laboratory and its potential effect on casework. J. Forensic Ident. 56, 558.

Prieto, L., Haned, H., Mosquera, A., Crespillo, M., Alemañ, M., Aler, M., et al., 2014. Euroforgen-NoE collaborative exercise on LRmix to demonstrate standardization of the interpretation of complex DNA profiles. Forensic Sci. Int. Genet. 9, 47–54.

Queen v. Sean Hoey, 2007. Neutral Citation Number 49 [2007] NICC, http://www.courtsni.gov.uk/en-gb/judicial%20decisions/publishedbyyear/documents/2007/2007%20nicc%2049/j_j_wei7021final.htm

Rand, S., Schürenkamp, M., Hohoff, C., Brinkmann, B., 2004. The GEDNAP blind trial concept. Part II. Trends and developments. Int. J. Leg. Med. 118, 83–89.

Raymond, J.J., van Oorschot, R.A., Gunn, P.R., Walsh, S.J., Roux, C., 2009. Trace evidence characteristics of DNA: a preliminary investigation of the persistence of DNA at crime scenes. Forensic Sci. Int. Genet. 4, 26–33.

Regina v. Dean Charles Cleobury, 2012. Neutral Citation Number [2012] EWCA Crim 17.

Regina v. Dlugosz, 2013. Neutral Citation Number: [2013] EWCA Crim 2, http://www.bailii.org/ew/cases/ewca/crim/2013/2.html

Regina v. Doheny and Adams, [1997] 1 Crim App R 369.

Regina v. Henderson, 2010. Neutral Citation Number. EWCA Crim 1269.

Regina v. Kerby, 2011. Central Criminal Court, date 2.3.2011 (unreported).

Regina v. Reed and Reed, Regina v. Garmson, 2009 [2009] EWCA Crim 2698, http://www.bailii.org/ew/cases/EWCA/Crim/2009/2698.html

Regina v. Weller, 2010. Neutral Citation Number [2010] EWCA Crim 1085.

Rennison, A., 2012. Report into the circumstances of a complaint received from the Greater Manchester Police on 7 March 2012 regarding DNA evidence provided by LGC forensics, http://www.homeoffice.gov.uk/publications/agencies-public-bodies/fsr/dna-contam-report?view=Binary

Rutty, G., Hopwood, A., Tucker, V., 2003. The effectiveness of protective clothing in the reduction of potential DNA contamination of the scene of crime. Int. J. Leg. Med. 117, 170–174.

Schneider, P., 2009. Expansion of the European standard set of DNA database loci—the current situation. Profiles in DNA 12(1), 6–7.

Schurr, B., (2012). Expert witnesses and the duties of disclosure and impartiality: the lessons of the IRA cases in England, http://www.aic.gov.au/media_library/conferences/medicine/schurr.pdf

Szkuta, B., Harvey, M.L., Ballantyne, K.N., van Oorschot, R.A.H., 2013. The potential transfer of trace DNA via high risk vectors during exhibit examination. Forensic Sci. Int. Genet. Suppl. Ser. 4, e55–e56.

Tamariz, J., Voynarovska, K., Prinz, M., Caragine, T., 2006. The application of ultraviolet irradiation to exogenous sources of DNA in plastic-ware and water for the amplification of low copy number DNA. J. Forensic Sci. 51, 790–794.

The Conti-Vecchiotti Report, 2011, http://knoxdnareport.wordpress.com/

The Hellman-Zanetti Report—on the acquittal of Amanda Knox and Raffaele Sollecito, translated into English, 2011, http://hellmannreport.wordpress.com/contents/reasons-for-the-decision/expert-review-of-exhibits-36-and-165b/

Thompson, W., Taroni, F., Aitken, C., 2003. How the probability of a false positive affects the value of DNA evidence. J. Forensic Sci. 48, 47–54.

Toothman, M.H., Kester, K.M., Champagne, J., Cruz, T.D., Street IV, W.S., Brown, B.L., 2008. Characterization of human DNA in environmental samples. Forensic Sci. Int. 178, 7–15.

UK National DNA Database, 2013, https://www.gov.uk/government/publications/national-dna-database-statistics

Vandewoestyne, M., Van Hoofstat, D., De Groote, S., Van Thuyne, N., Haerinck, S., Van Nieuwerburgh, F., et al. 2011. Sources of DNA contamination and decontamination procedures in the forensic laboratory. Int. J. Forensic Pract. Res. 2, https://biblio.ugent.be/input/download?func=downloadFile&recordOId=1891149&fileOId=1891151

van Oorschot, R.A., Ballantyne, K.N., Mitchell, R.J., 2010. Forensic trace DNA: a review. Investig. Genet. 1, 14.

Vincent, F., 2010. Report—inquiry into the circumstances that led to the conviction of Mr. Farah Abdulkadir Jama, https://assets.justice.vic.gov.au/justice/resources/4cd228fd-f61d-4449-b655-ad98323c4ccc/vincentreportfinal6may2010.pdf

Weir, B.S., 2006. The rarity of DNA profiles. Ann. Appl. Stat. 1, 358–370.

Witt, N., Rodger, G., Vandesompele, J., Benes, V., Zumla, A., Rook, G.A., et al. 2009. An assessment of air as a source of DNA contamination encountered when performing PCR. J. Biomol. Tech. 20, 236.

CPSIA information can be obtained
at www.ICGtesting.com
Printed in the USA
FFOW02n1607290915
17302FF